The Nature Detective Series

WILD FLOWERS
Learning to Identify

Pamela Forey

Illustrated by Cecilia Fitzsimons
Series Editor Lionel Bender

Macdonald

This book was designed and produced
by The Oregon Press Ltd, Faraday House,
8-10 Charing Cross Road, London WC2H 0HG for
Macdonald & Co. (Publishers) Ltd, Maxwell House,
Worship Street, London EC2A 2EN

Series conceived, designed and edited by
Lionel Bender, 10 Chelmsford Square,
London NW10 3AR, assisted by Madeleine Bender

© Lionel Bender 1984

ISBN 0-356-09712-9

Printed and bound by William Collins Sons
& Co. Ltd, Glasgow

CONTENTS

How to use this book	4
Where and when to look for plants	6
Clues and evidence	8
How plants work	14
Introduction to Ready reference and Fact file sections	16
Key/Ready reference section	18
Habitat fact files	30
Practical section	72
Recommended sites	78
Further reading/Glossary/Index	79

4 How to use this book

This book is not, and is not intended to be, a comprehensive field guide to wild flowers. It is rather a guide to the places in which wild flowering plants grow, with clues to help you find these habitats, and to many interesting species that grow in them. Although some of our commonest plants grow anywhere and everywhere, many others are common only in one or two selected habitats, and you need to know where to look for them.

The book is split into several sections designed to lead from a general discussion of where and how plants live to detailed studies of the major plant families and some of the most familiar habitats. Finally a practical section provides suggestions and ideas for field work and information to help you become an active member of the conservation movement which aims to preserve our wild plants and animals.

Where and when to look for plants, pages 6-7
In this section an appraisal is made of some of the factors which influence the growth of plants. Climate, soil type, amount of light and so on, greatly influence the number and type of plants you may expect to find in any one area. Seasons are also examined and a description is given of the changes which occur in the vegetation from early spring to autumn. It is possible to identify some flowering plants even when they are not in bloom!

Clues and evidence, pages 8-13
Following on from the previous section, four imaginary scenes illustrate the sort of places where particular plants are likely to be found. A list of key locations accompanying each scene identifies the many different types of microhabitats, where small changes in light, soil fertility and amount of water etc., lead to changes in the species growing. The plant examples shown in the scenes are illustrated and described in greater detail later in the book.

How plants work, pages 14-15
This section provides necessary background information to help you to understand the life of plants. Details are given of the functions of roots, stems and leaves as well as of the structure and function of flowers and fruits.

Introduction to Ready reference and Fact files sections, pages 16-17
Here are described the structure and ways to use the two main 'detective' sections of the book. In addition you will find illustrated explanations of many of the terms used to describe leaves and flowers in the following sections of the book.

Ready reference section, pages 18-29
This section deals with the major groupings of flowering plants you are likely to find. It begins with a simple key in which a series of clues will help you to place any particular plant in its correct botanical family. In the rest of the section, the families of flowering plants are described individually, with clues to help you to identify them, details of leaves and flowers, and with an illustration of one common member of each family.

How to use this book

Fact files section, pages 30-71
This, the longest section of the book, illustrates the most important common habitats to be found in Britain and continental Europe, together with some of the more familiar flowering plant species to be found in them. The ready reference and fact files sections are intended to complement each other, with the emphasis on the plant families in the first and on the habitats here in the second. Together the two sections will help you to build up an 'identikit picture' of the plant world in this country, with more than 150 species of flowering plants being described and illustrated.

Practical section, pages 72-77
These pages look at some of the projects you could undertake in your garden or in the field to increase your understanding of wild flowers and their habitats. Suggestions for areas of study, a checklist of the equipment you will need and details of methods are all included. Hints are given on how to keep your records, and ways in which you can help to conserve plants and animals are explained. Finally, there is a list of addresses of some important organizations concerned with conservation and the countryside.

Recommended sites, page 78
Details are given of many of the richest wild flower areas in Britain. An attempt has been made to include sites that illustrate all the habitats described in the fact files section, but there may not be a classic site near you. This does not mean that you cannot see wild flowers or do field work. The commonest habitats are those like woodland and hedgerows which occur throughout the British Isles.

Further reading, page 79
Included here are a list of recommended books that will expand your knowledge of wild plants. They vary from field guides useful or identification of all flowering plants, to more detailed books on plant habitats, biology and folklore.

Glossary, page 79
Here are defined some of the botanical terms used in the book. Also in this small section page references are given for the more general botanical topics which are explained and/or illustrated in detail on other pages.

Index, pages 79-80
The index provides an immediate page guide to information on each species considered in the book.

Wild flowers – learning to identify will help you to find wild plants wherever you live. But conservation must be the key word in any approach to the natural world. So please do not pick the flowers or trample them or damage their habitats. And never dig them up. Leave them where they are so that our world will remain a beautiful, varied and healthy world to live in.

6 Where and when to look for plants

The discussion that follows is concerned less with the detailed practicalities of plant spotting, which you will find on pages 72 to 77, than with generally where and when to look for flowering plants. Next time you investigate a wood or walk alongside a hedge, notice the many different tiny environments or microhabitats and the different plants in each. A sunny gateway has one group of plants – knotgrass and dock, for example – while a shady damp place has another – bugle and celandines are particularly common. Another spot such as beneath a large tree is also shady but here the ground is dry and little grows but moss and violets in spring. An experiment that can be fun is to compare the south sunny side of a hedge with the north shady side. You will often find quite different plants on the two sides. In the fact files and clues and evidence sections of this book there are clear indications as to the habitat preferences of the plants selected which will help you to decide where it is most likely to find them.

Climate This is an important factor in plant distribution even in a small island like ours. The south of Britain has an annual average temperature a few degrees higher than the north while the west is warmer and wetter than the east. You may not be able to travel to the south and north of the country to see the resulting change in vegetation but you should be able to see changes in climate and vegetation in your own immediate area. For instance, if you live on a hill you will almost certainly be able to see differences in vegetation which occur from one side to the other, especially if the prevailing wind blows across the hill. The wind drops its rain on the first exposed hillside while the far side is in a 'rain shadow' – it is much drier and more sheltered. Vegetation changes may be considerable. Even tiny differences in climate (microclimate) affect plant growth. Look at the trees in your garden. You will find that there is moss growing on the cooler damper northern sides of the trees and little or no moss on the hotter drier southern sides.

Soil Plants are very often particular about the texture and pH – a measure of the acidity or alkalinity – of the soil in which they grow. Take a look at the soil in your garden. If it is made of large loose particles then it is a light sandy soil with an open texture. Water drains through it quickly taking the soil nutrients (dissolved salts) with it. Your soil will be dry in summer but well-drained in winter. It will be low in plant food – a hungry sterile soil. If your soil is made of tiny particles, because these tend to cling together, it will be dense and heavy – a clay soil. It will retain its water in summer but will be badly drained and waterlogged in winter. However, it will be rich in plant nutrients. Often the soil in your garden will be a mixture of sand and clay, a loam.

The second important factor of the soil is its pH. Plants are very sensitive to pH levels and can be divided into acid-loving and alkali (base)-loving types. If you know that a plant grows on acid sandy soils like those of some moorlands then you do not look for it on alkaline clay soils. If you know that a plant is a lime-lover then you look for it on alkaline soils like those found on the calcareous limestone and chalk downlands. (Lime contains calcium, one of the most common minerals in an alkaline soil.) Clay soils may be acid or alkaline depending on the rock below.

In the fact files, pages 30-71, you will find many clues to the soil preferences of the plants described. In the practical section, on page 73, are details of how you can test the soil for pH.

Where and when to look for plants

Seasonal changes Knowing the preference of a plant for a heavy soil, a shady spot or extra water at its roots does not guarantee that you will be able to locate and identify it unless you know something of its seasonal changes. The changing of the seasons brings a major transformation, especially from winter to spring and summer, but in reality there is a continuous subtle day-to-day change in the growth, flowering, fruit formation and decay of many plants.

Spring In early spring the ground may be almost bare or covered by an apparently dead mat of grasses. Often the earliest flowering plants to appear are those that have a food store underground – a bulb or tuber, for example. Species like snowdrops or bluebells can start into growth almost before winter has ended since their food store gives them a head start over those species that rely solely on the sun for their food (see page 14). Another group of plants conspicuous in spring are the over-wintering annuals, like the chickweeds in your garden. These plants germinate from seeds in the autumn, remain as small green plants through the winter and flower in the spring. Many would go unnoticed in the dense summer growth but in spring they show up as welcome splashes of green.

One of the most tantalising aspects of spring are the many summer-flowering plants which form clumps or mats of leaves at this season. There are two ways of finding out what they are. Either you can ask an expert (see page 77), or you can watch the plants as they develop flower buds until finally comes the day when the first buds open. At this point you can attempt some nature detective work and using the various sections in this book try to identify the plant for yourself. You will soon become quite expert at this fascinating past-time and next spring you will recognize the plants before they flower.

Summer is the season when there are so many plants in flower that everywhere you look something else seems to have come into bloom. Look for early summer-flowering plants like cow parsley, midsummer flowers like meadowsweet and late summer blooms of the daisy family. You will find details of flowering times given for all the plants in the fact files.

As the summer progresses, more and more flowers are replaced by fruits (see page 15) until finally, in autumn, most of the plants are in fruit and only a few late blooms remain. The fruits are as individual as the flowers and are just as useful in identifying the plant if you know how to recognize them. You will find illustrations of the fruits in the fact files and ready reference sections and on page 15. One of the best ways of learning which fruit belongs to which plant is to watch the development as you did with leaves and buds in spring. Fortunately many plants develop their first fruits while the later flowers are still blooming, which makes recognition easier.

Winter Gradually even the fruits disappear and the autumn becomes winter. At this time of year there is not much to see. Most of the plants are dormant, either overwintering as seeds or as protected crowns, creeping stems or bulbs, all under the ground. Above ground are dead leaves, rotting stems and empty seed pods making a mat of dead vegetation which may be covered by snow. The dormant plants are protected, insulated against frost by these layers, so that when spring comes they are still alive and ready to begin another season of growth.

8 Clues and evidence – Woodlands and hedgerows

The panoramas below and on the following four pages illustrate some of the best places to look for wild plants. The key locations provide clues to help you decide which plants are most likely to be found in which situations.

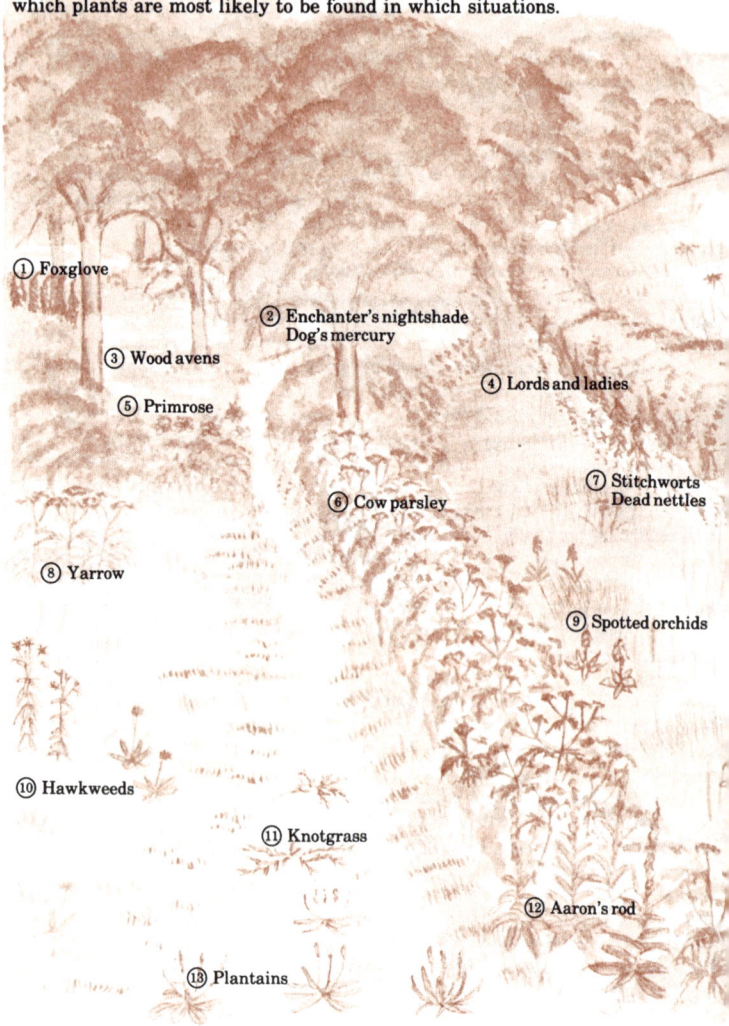

① Foxglove
② Enchanter's nightshade / Dog's mercury
③ Wood avens
④ Lords and ladies
⑤ Primrose
⑥ Cow parsley
⑦ Stitchworts / Dead nettles
⑧ Yarrow
⑨ Spotted orchids
⑩ Hawkweeds
⑪ Knotgrass
⑫ Aaron's rod
⑱ Plantains

Grassland 9

Key locations
Woodland clearings 1, 3, 5, 14, 15, 16
Shady woodland 2, 3, 4, 5
Base of hedgerows 3, 4, 5, 6, 7, 11, 14, 16
Roadside verges 8, 10, 11, 13, 18, 23, 28, 29
Grassy paths 8, 10, 11, 13, 18
Grassy banks 6, 10, 12, 13, 18, 23, 27, 28
Wet meadows 9, 10, 17, 18, 24, 25, 26, 28
Hayfields 9, 17, 18, 27, 28, 29
Dry walls 19, 20, 21, 23
Base of walls 5, 7, 23
Gates 11, 13, 15, 21, 22

(14) Alkanet and others of the mint family
(15) Jack-by-the-hedge Hogweed
(16) Thistles Campions
(17) Sorrels Poppies
(18) Buttercups Daisies
(19) Stonecrops
(20) Pellitory-of-the-wall
(21) Bindweeds
(22) Docks
(23) Herb robert Bedstraws
(24) Cuckoo flower
(25) Lousewort
(26) Devil's-bit scabious
(27) Cowslips
(28) Vetches
(29) Clovers

10 Clues and evidence – Gardens and wasteland

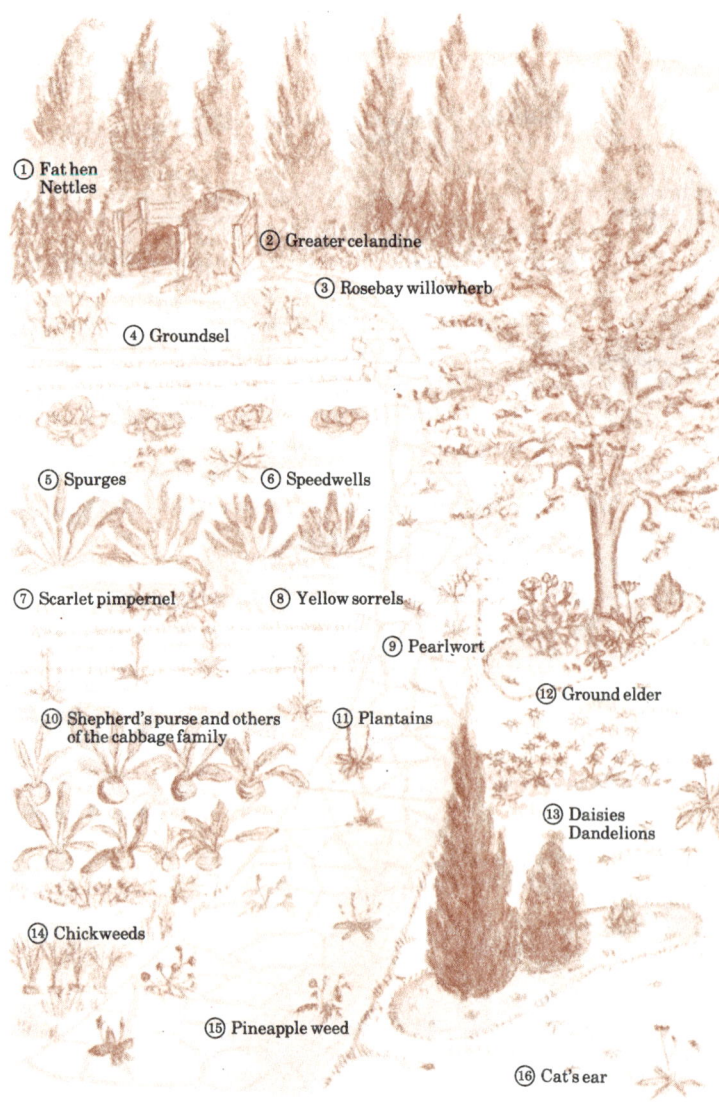

Gardens and wasteland 11

Key locations
Hedgerows 1, 2, 3, 6, 12, 17, 21, 22, 24, 26, 30, 31
Vegetable and flower gardens 1, 4, 5, 6, 7, 8, 10, 12, 14, 21, 25
Paths and tracks 9, 11, 15, 16, 28, 31
Lawns 11, 13, 16, 19, 22, 31
Wire fences 18, 27
Brick rubble 4, 17, 18, 20, 23, 24, 25, 29
Open ground 4, 5, 7, 13, 20, 22, 25, 26, 28, 31
Around old buildings 1, 17, 18, 20, 21, 23, 27
Damp areas 28, 29, 30, 31

12 Clues and evidence – Water and waterside

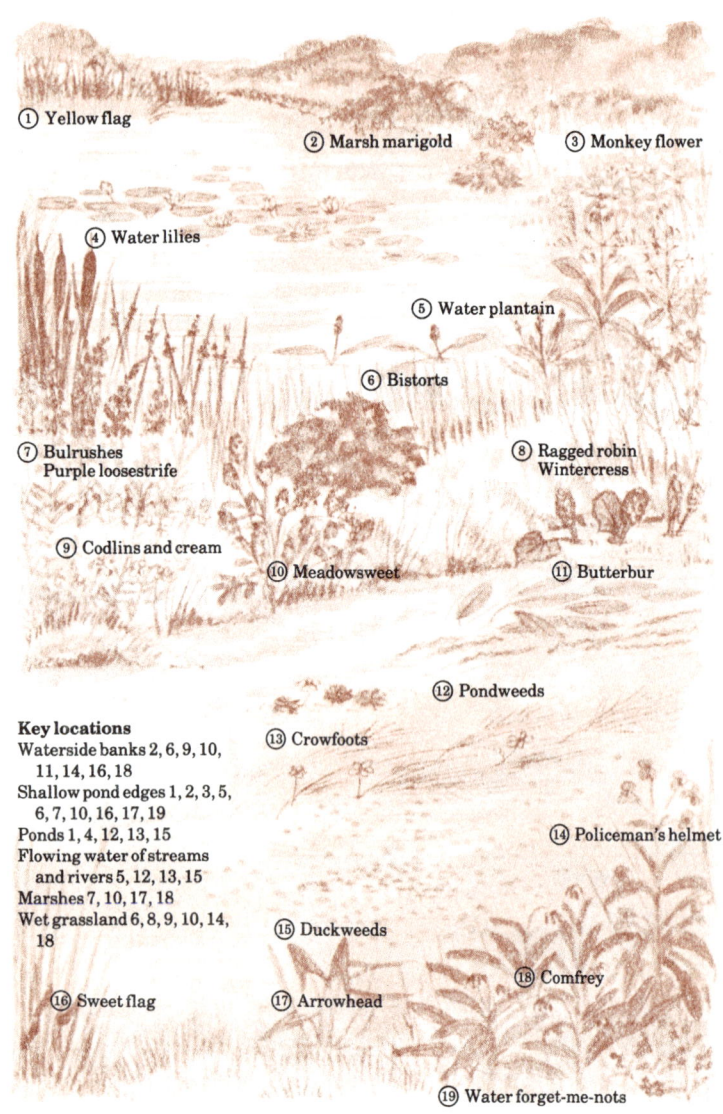

① Yellow flag
② Marsh marigold
③ Monkey flower
④ Water lilies
⑤ Water plantain
⑥ Bistorts
⑦ Bulrushes
  Purple loosestrife
⑧ Ragged robin
  Wintercress
⑨ Codlins and cream
⑩ Meadowsweet
⑪ Butterbur
⑫ Pondweeds
⑬ Crowfoots
⑭ Policeman's helmet
⑮ Duckweeds
⑯ Sweet flag
⑰ Arrowhead
⑱ Comfrey
⑲ Water forget-me-nots

Key locations
Waterside banks 2, 6, 9, 10, 11, 14, 16, 18
Shallow pond edges 1, 2, 3, 5, 6, 7, 10, 16, 17, 19
Ponds 1, 4, 12, 13, 15
Flowing water of streams and rivers 5, 12, 13, 15
Marshes 7, 10, 17, 18
Wet grassland 6, 8, 9, 10, 14, 18

Seashore; dunes and shingle banks 13

① Ragwort
② Lady's bedstraw
③ Thyme
④ Restharrow
⑤ Bindweeds
⑥ Storksbill
⑦ Marram grass
⑧ Sea sandwort
⑨ Sea wormwood
⑩ Sea rocket
⑪ Sea beet
⑫ Sea campion
⑬ Oraches
⑭ Scentless mayweed
⑮ Knotgrass

Key locations
Fixed dunes 1, 2, 3, 4, 6
Foredunes 7, 8, 9, 15
Driftlines 10, 11, 13
Shingle banks 1, 5, 9, 11, 12, 13, 14, 15
Paths and tracks 13, 15

14   How plants work

Plants come in a variety of forms from tiny creeping annuals which live only for a season to the giant redwood trees of California which live for thousands of years. This book is concerned with herbs, the small flowering plants. These are not woody like trees or shrubs and, in this country at least, their leafy stems die back to the ground each winter or they survive as seeds. To understand the life of such a plant it is useful to look at its four major parts – roots, stems, leaves and flowers.

Roots These grow underground, anchoring the plant to the earth and absorbing water from the soil together with the dissolved salts that the plant needs to grow and stay healthy.

Stems The stem forms the link between roots and leaves. Stems are much more variable than roots. They may be creeping above or below the ground, strong and erect, weak and straggling, branched or unbranched. In some plants, like those which have rosettes of leaves, the stems may be very short and the leaves appear to grow directly from the roots. Inside the stems are bundles of special long cells, joined end to end, which are responsible for carrying water absorbed by the roots up to the top of the plant (this is true even of the highest tree) and to the leaves.

Leaves The leaves are the 'power-house' of the plant. In them the plant's food is manufactured. In winter, when a plant loses its leaves, it must remain dormant, conserving its energy until spring returns. Then the plant unfolds new leaves and starts making food again. It is rather like a mammal in hibernation.

Plants manufacture their food by a complicated process called photosynthesis. This involves the green pigment (chlorophyll) in the leaves which traps the energy of sunlight and uses this power to combine carbon dioxide (a gas from the air which enters the leaves through special airholes) with water to make sugars. The sugars can be transformed into starch for storage. Proteins required for cell growth and repair are formed by combining the sugars with nitrogen compounds absorbed from the soil with the water. The foods are transported to all parts of the plant by bundles of long cells in the stems, like those which transport the water.

Flowers are borne at certain times of the year, varying according to species. Flowering times are given for all the plants described in the fact files section of this book pp. 30-71, but may change considerably depending on whether the specimen is in southern England or northern Scotland.

A typical flower has four separate rings or whorls of flower parts. The outermost parts are the sepals – usually green and leaflike, protecting the flower in bud

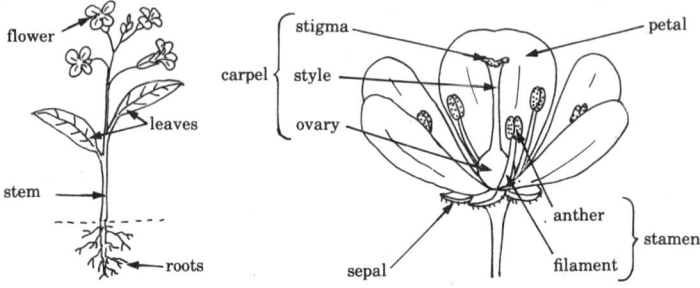

How plants work

and sometimes the fruit. Next are the petals, usually brightly coloured and often sweetly scented to attract insects for pollination. The next whorl consists of stamens – long stalks or filaments topped by anthers which contain the pollen grains (male sex cells). The fourth and innermost whorl is formed by carpels which contain the female egg cells. Each carpel consists of an ovary at the base containing eggs, a tubular style and a stigma at the top on which the pollen lands. Some plants bear flowers of one sex only, either male or female. The flowers in many genera are enclosed or cupped in green leaflike structures called bracts.

Pollen grains are carried by wind or by insects from one flower to another. This is the process of *pollination*. Pollen grains land on the stigma and, if they are from the same species of plant, grow down the tubular style into the ovary where the male sex cells join with the eggs. These fertilized eggs develop into seeds, and the carpels grow with them to form the fruits.

Fruits There are an enormous number of different kinds of fruits, most of them adapted to help dispersal of the seeds contained within. If all the seeds germinated around the parent plant they would compete for space, water etc., so dispersal lessens the competition and helps to spread the species. If the fruit is single-seeded, then the fruit and seed form a single structure and are dispersed together. The fruits of the daisy family are of this type; many have 'parachutes' of hairs which catch the wind and carry the fruits far from the parent plant. Fruits dispersed by animals may be hooked, like those of avens or burdock, so that they cling to fur or feathers and are carried away. Berries are fruits which attract animals usually by their bright colour. The fruits are eaten and the seeds are left on the ground or pass through the animals unharmed. Some fruits use mechanical means to aid seed dispersal. Capsules are many-seeded fruits which split open by a variety of mechanisms – poppy capsules are like pepper shakers, throwing out seeds with every swing in the wind. The pods of many members of the pea family twist as they split and the seeds are flung out. Many of the different fruits are shown below, others are illustrated in the ready reference and fact file sections.

Growth cycles Flowering plants may have one of several life cycles. Annuals germinate from seed, develop into mature flowering plants, set seed and die, all within one season or year. Biennial plants germinate from seed to form a leafy plant in the first year and produce flowers, set seed and die in the second year, taking two years to complete their life span. Perennial plants live from year to year, surviving the winters beneath the ground, losing their leaves each year.

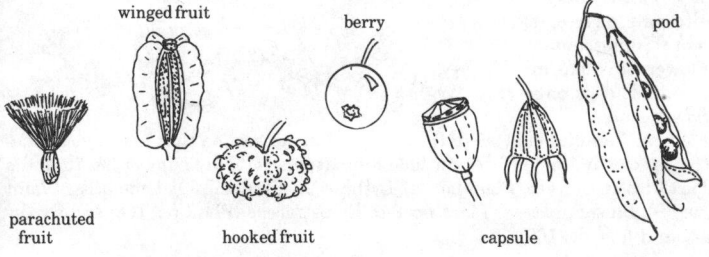

parachuted fruit — winged fruit — hooked fruit — berry — capsule — pod

16 Introduction to Ready reference and Fact files

In these, the two largest sections of the book, plants are examined from two rather different points of view. The ready reference section, pp. 18-29, deals with 44 of the major families of flowering plants to be found in Britain and continental Europe. The second section, the fact files, looks at 21 of the habitats in which plants grow and some of the flowering species most typical of those habitats.

Ready reference Lack of space makes it impossible to include all the plant families present in Britain (there are well over 100 of them) and not all the families of plants mentioned in the fact files section are included. In general, families that have been omitted are those with few species, where the only common species is described and illustrated in the fact files. You will find a list of such families at the bottom of this page. Grasses, sedges and rushes have also been left out – they are so numerous that they would fill a book of this size alone.

You should be able to assign a plant to a family by using the key on page 18. The text for each family consists of a few general comments including any facts of particular interest, characteristics of stems and leaves, flowers and fruits. There is then an illustration of one of the common members of the family. The numbers included at the end of each text block refer to species within the fact files which also belong to this family.

Fact files Twenty-one typical British and European habitats are included. There is a brief introduction to each one and six of the commonest species are described and illustrated. All species grow throughout Europe unless otherwise stated. The figures given as 'up to 60 cm', for example, is a reference to the average typical height of the plant growing in its normal habitat.

Plant description In both sections you will find many inevitable references to plant anatomy. Although one has tried to keep the use of botanical terms to a minimum, some use of them is essential, especially when referring to leaves and flowers. You will find here and on the page facing, seven more plant species which, between them, illustrate the majority of the terms you will encounter in the text. Other terms are explained in the glossary on page 79. A description and diagram of the parts of the flower, together with their functions, are given on pages 14-15. In the field such features are major clues to the identity of a plant.

1. White stonecrop
Sedum album
Leaves simple,
succulent or fleshy,
alternate, on creeping,
mat-forming stems.
Flowers star-like, in
terminal heads, on erect
flower-stalks.

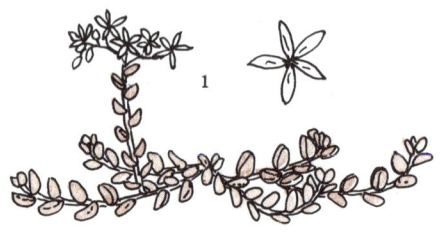

Footnote Families omitted in the Ready reference section that have representative species in the Fact files include Fumariaceae (Plants number 36, 76 in the Fact files), Cistaceae (Plant no. 44), Lythraceae (Plant no. 59), Lemnaceae (Plant no. 69), Balsaminaceae (Plant no. 94), Empetraceae (Plant no. 108) and Cyperaceae (Plant no. 109).

17

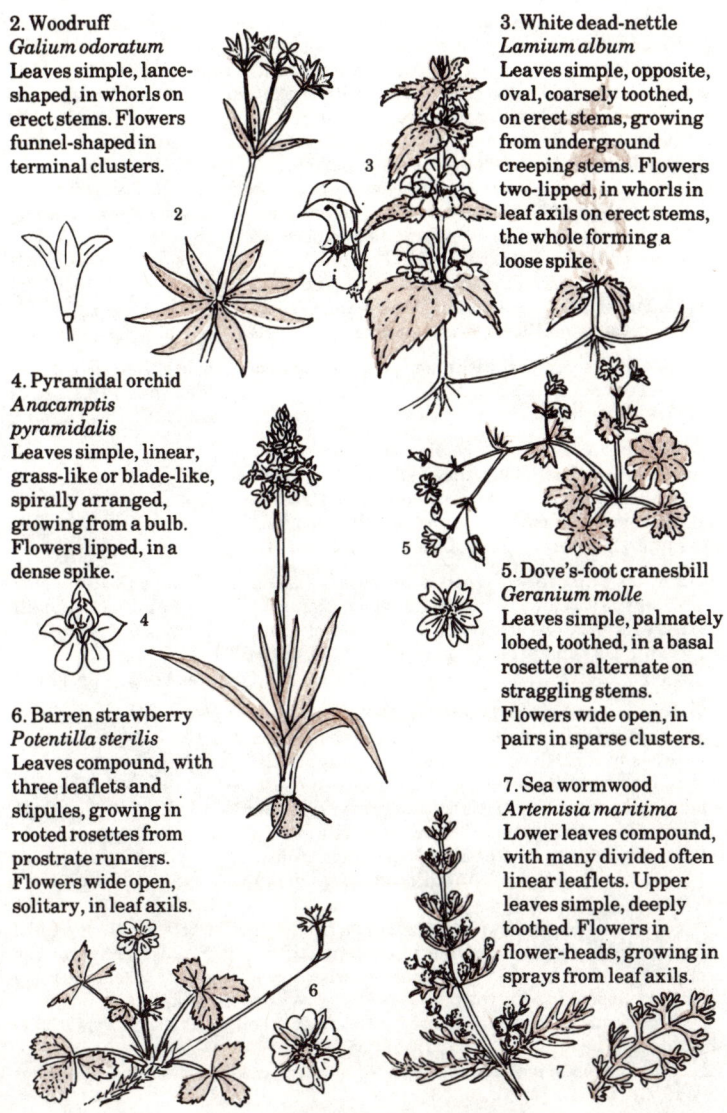

2. Woodruff
Galium odoratum
Leaves simple, lance-shaped, in whorls on erect stems. Flowers funnel-shaped in terminal clusters.

3. White dead-nettle
Lamium album
Leaves simple, opposite, oval, coarsely toothed, on erect stems, growing from underground creeping stems. Flowers two-lipped, in whorls in leaf axils on erect stems, the whole forming a loose spike.

4. Pyramidal orchid
Anacamptis pyramidalis
Leaves simple, linear, grass-like or blade-like, spirally arranged, growing from a bulb. Flowers lipped, in a dense spike.

5. Dove's-foot cranesbill
Geranium molle
Leaves simple, palmately lobed, toothed, in a basal rosette or alternate on straggling stems. Flowers wide open, in pairs in sparse clusters.

6. Barren strawberry
Potentilla sterilis
Leaves compound, with three leaflets and stipules, growing in rooted rosettes from prostrate runners. Flowers wide open, solitary, in leaf axils.

7. Sea wormwood
Artemisia maritima
Lower leaves compound, with many divided often linear leaflets. Upper leaves simple, deeply toothed. Flowers in flower-heads, growing in sprays from leaf axils.

18 Key to families

You should be able to assign a plant to its family by using this key. However, plants do not always obey the rules that we make for them and a key can only be completely accurate if it is very complicated (and many pages long). We have tried to make a simple key that will guide you to the right family most of the time. The most common problems that you are likely to encounter are noted at the bottom of the page. To use the key, work through the list of options. Each offers two or more choices. Reading across a line, where a number in bold type is indicated move on to this option. Where a group of families and a page number is indicated, move on to the relevant page(s) and check the family descriptions until you find one that fits.

(1) Leaves with parallel veins and flower parts in threes or multiples of this number .... **Families 1-8, pages 19-20**

(1) Leaves with netted veins and flower parts in twos, fours or fives or multiples of these numbers **2**

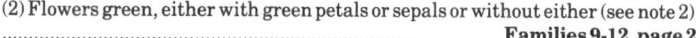

(2) Flowers green, either with green petals or sepals or without either (see note 2) .... **Families 9-12, page 21**

(2) Flowers with coloured (not green) petals **3**

(3) Flowers in which the petals are separate, not joined into a tube (although the sepals may be joined) .... **Families 13-32, go to 4**

(3) Flowers with petals all joined together, more or less forming a tube .... **Families 29-44, go to 5**

(4) Flowers with two or four petals (see note 3) .... **Families 13-15, page 22**
(4) Flowers with many petals (25-30), water plants .... **Family 16, page 22**
(4) Flowers usually with five petals (some species may have four petals, see note 3, and families 17 and 19 have some species with 5-10 petals) ....
.... **Families 17-32, pages 23-26**

(5) Flowers bell-shaped, tubular or one- or two-lipped, often large and showy, not usually tiny and in dense heads .... **Families 32-41, page 26-29**
(5) Flowers usually small, mostly in heads, dense spikes or clusters. The heads of flowers may give the impressions of being one flower, as in the daisy family (44) .... **Families 29-31, page 26 and Families 40-44, page 29**

Notes

(1) You will notice that in several places there is an overlap between the groups of families; this is because families have many different genera. In using this key you may be guided to the right family by either sequence of options, but the route will vary depending on which species you have in your hand.

(2) Some families have one or two species with green petal-less flowers. These include families 2, 3, 4, 15, 17, 19, 23, 35, 44.

(3) Some families have one or two species with four petals. These include families 17, 19, 20, 23, 24, 32, 35, 36, 39, 41, 42, 43.

Ready reference – Flowering plant families i

1 Alismataceae Water plantain family
Very small family of water plants. *Leaves* lance-shaped or rounded with long stalks; many growing in a clump or floating on the water. *Flowers* in sparse clusters on leafless flower stalks; wide open with three free sepals and petals. Fruits in small round clusters or whorls. *Example* Arrow-head *Sagittaria sagittifolia*. See 72.

2 Potamogetonaceae Pondweed family
Very small family of water plants, often grown in aquaria and ponds.
Leaves linear, lance-shaped or rounded, with large stipules; totally submerged or floating on the water.
Flowers borne in green spikes below the water; petals and sepals absent. One-seeded green fruits borne in fruiting spikes, projecting above the surface of the water.
Example Curled pondweed *Potamogeton crispus*. See 68.

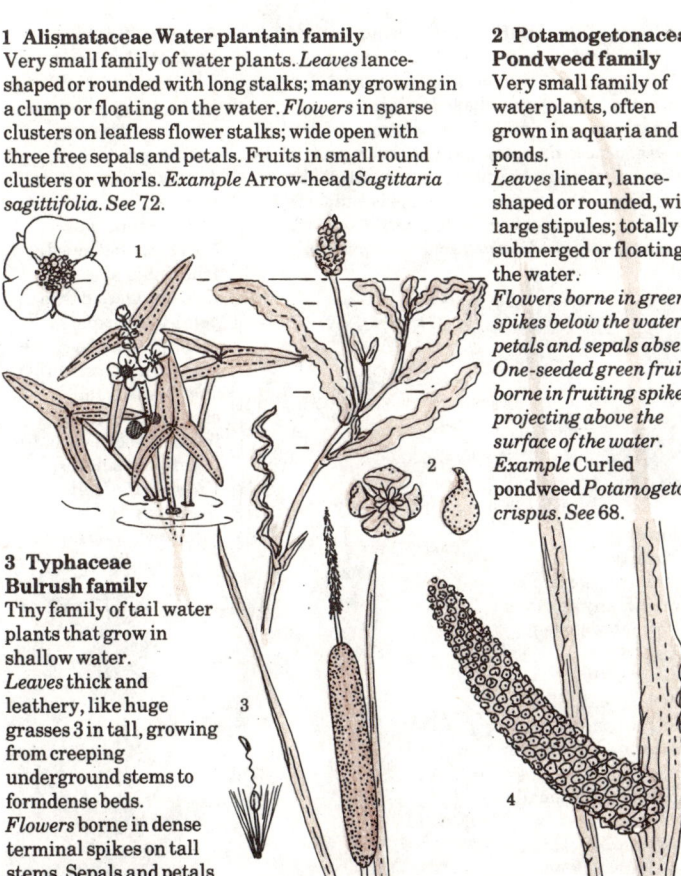

3 Typhaceae Bulrush family
Tiny family of tall water plants that grow in shallow water.
Leaves thick and leathery, like huge grasses 3 in tall, growing from creeping underground stems to form dense beds.
Flowers borne in dense terminal spikes on tall stems. Sepals and petals absent, flowers scaly or hairy instead, male and female flowers separate. Fruits dry in dense spikes, eventually splitting open to release the seeds.
Example Lesser reedmace *Typha angustifolia*. See 56.

4 Araceae Arum family
Relatively large family of herbs, some of which are very poisonous. *Leaves* often large, arrow-shaped with long stalks or like large grasses, up to 1 m tall. *Flowers* very distinctive. Male and female flowers separate in a dense spike, usually sheathed in a spathe and followed by a spike of brightly coloured, often poisonous berries. *Example* Sweet flag *Acorus calamus*. See 15.

Ready reference – Flowering plant families ii

5 Liliaceae Lily family (Onion family)
Large family of herbs, many grown as vegetables (e.g. onions) or in flower gardens (e.g. tulips). *Leaves* often grass-like or lance-shaped on leafy stems, growing from underground creeping stems or bulbs. *Flowers* borne in drooping sprays or heads on leafless flower stalks or terminating leafy stems; bed-shaped or star-like with three petal-like sepals and three petals, free or united. Fruits are capsules or berries. *Example* Bog asphodel *Narthecium ossifragum*. See 2, 5

6 Amaryllidaceae Daffodil family
Small family of bulbous herbs, many grown in flower gardens (e.g. snowdrops). *Leaves* grass-like, growing from an underground bulb. *Flowers* bell-shaped or trumpet-shaped with three petals and three petal-like sepals, sometimes in the shape of a corona; borne either singly or in small clusters on leafless flower stalks. Fruits are usually capsules. *Example* Daffodil *Narcissus pseudonarcissus*.

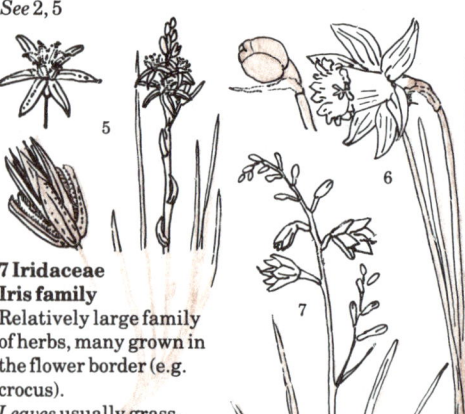

7 Iridaceae Iris family
Relatively large family of herbs, many grown in the flower border (e.g. crocus).
Leaves usually grass-like with sheath-like bases, growing from an underground stem, corm or bulb.
Flowers borne in small clusters or many-flowered spikes; three petal-like sepals and three petals may be all alike or in two dissimilar whorls. Fruits are capsules, opening by valves and usually bearing round scars on the tops.
Example Montbretia *Tritonia* × *crocosmiflora*. See 57.

8 Orchidaceae Orchid family
One of the largest families of flowering plants, mostly herbs and epiphytes. *Leaves* spirally arranged with sheathing bases; usually blade-like or lance-shaped, often with spots. *Flowers* in a more or less dense spike terminating a leafless flower stalk. Often strangely shaped and coloured; three sepals and petals, which may be petal-like or sepal-like. Fruits are capsules opening by slits and containing numerous tiny seeds. *Example* Twayblade *Listera ovata*. See 53 & p. 17(4).

Ready reference – Flowering plant families iii

9 Chenopodiaceae Goosefoot family
Small family of herbs and shrubs, often associated with wasteland and sea shores.
Leaves simple, alternate, often mealy in appearance or succulent, on branched stems.
Flowers borne in small clusters which are grouped into larger flowering shoots; with three to five greenish sepals or tiny and without sepals; petals absent. Fruits are one-seeded nuts which do not split open, often enclosed in sepals.
Example Herbaceous seablite *Suaeda maritima*. See 81, 95, 123, 124.

10 Euphorbiaceae Spurge family
Very large family of trees, shrubs and herbs, several of economic importance (e.g. castor oil plant). Many are poisonous. *Leaves* simple or compound, usually with stipules, alternate. Stems may have milky juice. *Flowers* tiny; petals and often sepals absent. In spurges the flowers are clustered above large greenish-yellow bracts which look like petals. Fruits are capsules. *Example* Petty spurge *Euphorbia peplus*. See 3, 83.

12 Plantaginaceae Plantain family
Very small family of herbs, mostly small rosette-forming plants.
Leaves simple, sometimes toothed, linear or lance-shaped, usually arranged in a rosette.
Flowers borne in dense spikes on leafless flower stalks; sepals green, petals membranous, neither as conspicuous as the sometimes brightly coloured anthers. Fruit a capsule opening by a lid, or one-seeded.
Example Great plantain *Plantago major*. See 87.

11 Urticaceae Nettle family
Small family of herbs and small shrubs. *Leaves* simple, often toothed, arranged in opposite pairs or alternately on the stems; with stipules and often with stinging hairs. *Flowers* in clusters in leaf axils; male and female separate, usually with tubular green sepals and no petals. Fruits usually one-seeded. *Example* Pellitory-of-the-wall *Parietaria judaica*. See 97.

Ready reference – Flowering plant families iv

13 Papaveraceae Poppy family
Very small family of herbs and shrubs, several of which are poisonous. Opium comes from the opium poppy. *Leaves* spirally arranged on the stems, often lobed or divided; stems contain a coloured milky sap. *Flowers* wide open with two or three free sepals and four free petals, soon falling off. Fruits are capsules opening by valves or pores, with many small seeds. *Example* Greater celandine *Chelidonium majus*. See 73.

14 Cruciferae Cabbage family
Large family of herbs, many of which are grown as vegetables (e.g. turnips) or spices (e.g. mustard).
Leaves spirally arranged on the stems, very variable, entire or divided.
Flowers in large branched leafy clusters; sepals and petals four, free, in the form of alternate crosses. Fruits distinctive, two-celled, usually with a central vertical partition, opening from the bottom.
Example Wintercress *Barbarea vulgaris*. See 21, 35, 49, 74, 84, 126.

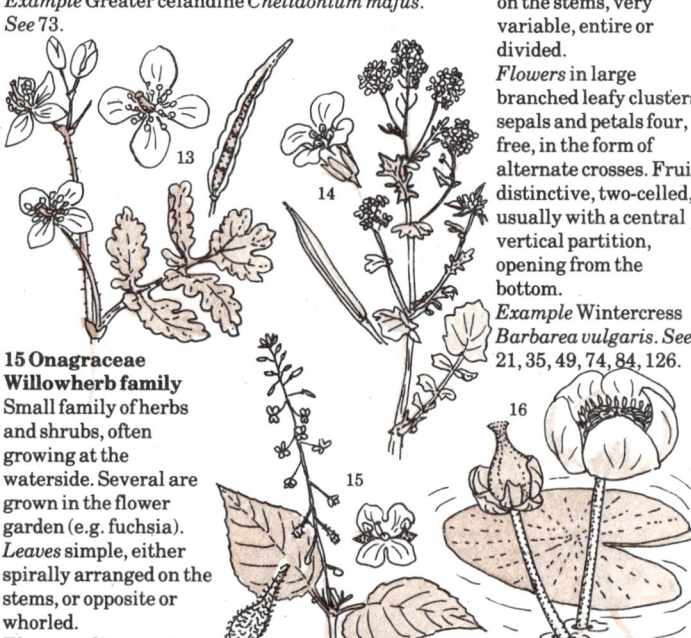

15 Onagraceae Willowherb family
Small family of herbs and shrubs, often growing at the waterside. Several are grown in the flower garden (e.g. fuchsia).
Leaves simple, either spirally arranged on the stems, or opposite or whorled.
Flowers solitary or in clusters in leaf axils; wide open; sepals and petals usually four, sometimes two or absent, soon falling. Fruits are usually capsules.
Example Enchanter's nightshade *Circaea lutetiana*. See 8, 58.

16 Nymphaeaceae Water lily family
Tiny family of water plants, often grown in ornamental ponds. *Leaves* thin and submerged or round and floating, with long stalks; growing from a creeping stem at the bottom of the pond. *Flowers* large and showy, solitary, growing on long stalks and floating on the surface; three to six sepals, many free petals and petal-like stamens (20 to 30). Fruit a spongy capsule or like a berry, submerged or floating on the water. *Example* Yellow water lily *Nuphar lutea*. See 67.

Ready reference – Flowering plant families v

17 Ranunculaceae Buttercup family

Large family of herbs and climbers. Most species have acrid sap and several are very poisonous. Many are grown in flower gardens (e.g. delphiniums). *Leaves* spirally arranged on the stems, or opposite; often palmate or dissected. *Flowers* wide open or spurred with five to ten free petals; sepals often five, sometimes petal-like or absent; stamens numerous. Fruits in one-seeded clusters or many-seeded pods. *Example* Columbine *Aquilegia vulgaris. See* 1, 18, 38, 61, 63, 71, 89.

18 Violaceae Violet family

Relatively large family of herbs and shrubs, several of which are grown in flower borders (e.g. pansies). *Leaves* simple with stipules, alternately arranged on the stems. *Flowering* wide open, solitary or in clusters; sepals and petals five, free, lowermost petals often larger and spurred. Fruits are capsules or berries. *Example* Sweet violet *Viola odorata. See* 6, 78.

19 Rosaceae Rose family

Large family of trees, shrubs and herbs, many of which are grown for their fruit (e.g. apples) or in flower borders (e.g. roses). *Leaves* simple or compound with stipules, arranged alternately on the stems. *Flowers* solitary or in spikes or clusters; wide open with five free sepals and petals (sometimes petals four or absent); stamens as many as petals or numerous; fruits very varied, dry or fleshy. *Example* Wood avens *Geum urbanum. See* 11, 28, 46, 55, 110, 115, 116 & p. 17(6).

20 Saxifragaceae Saxifrage family

Small family of herbs, many of them mountain plants. They are grown in flower borders (e.g. London pride) and on rock gardens. *Leaves* very variable; large and entire, large and compound or small and fleshy; often crowded into dense rosettes or clumps. *Flowers* usually small and star-like in many-flowered clusters on leafless flower stalks; sepals and petals, usually five, free (petals sometimes four or absent); stamens ten. Fruits are capsules. *Example* Purple saxifrage *Saxifraga oppositifolia. See* 118.

Ready reference – Flowering plant families vi

21 Hypericaceae St John's wort family
Small family of herbs, shrubs and trees, several of which are grown in flower gardens (e.g. rose of Sharon). *Leaves* simple, in opposite pairs, often dotted with glands; stems with resinous sap. *Flowers* often large, solitary or in small terminal clusters; sepals and petals five, free, with numerous stamens forming distinctive centres to the flowers. Fruits are capsules. *Example* Tutsan *Hypericum androsaemum*. See 9.

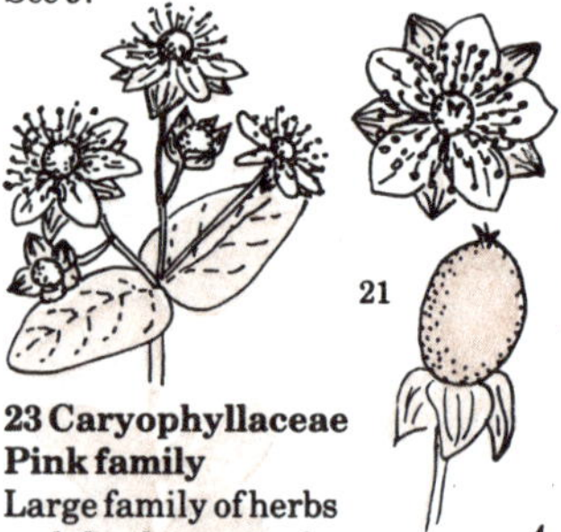

22 Papilionaceae Pea family
Very large family of herbs, shrubs and trees, many of which are grown as vegetables (e.g. benas). Their roots bear nitrogen-fixing bacteria which enrich the soil. *Leaves* with stipules, usually compound with three to many leaflets, sometimes ending in tendrils. *Flowers* very distinctive; five sepals joined into a tube; five unequal petals, the rear petal large and often erect, the two side petals forming 'wings' and the two lowest joined together. Fruits are pods, contianing several seeds. *Example* Restharrow *Ononis repens*. See 22, 39, 41, 45, 105.

23 Caryophyllaceae Pink family
Large family of herbs and shrubs, some of which are grown in flower borders (e.g. carnations). *Leaves* simple, frequently linear, in opposite pairs which are often joined together across the stem. *Flowers* wide open or minute, often in twos, terminating the flower stalks; sepals and petals four or five, sometimes petals absent or very small; sepals free or united into a tube, petals free. Stamens twice the number of petals. Fruits are capsules. *Example* Mouse-ear chickweed *Cerastium fontanum*. See 13, 14, 50, 79, 122, 125.

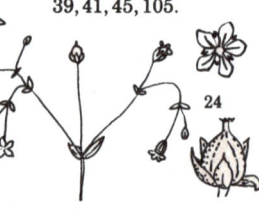

24 Linaceae Flax family
Small family of herbs, shrubs and trees, some of which are economically important as fibre- or oil-seed producing plants (e.g. flax, linseed). *Leaves* simple, linear or lance-shaped, arranged alternately or in opposite pairs on the stems. *Flowers* wide open, solitary or in clusters; sepals and petals five (sometimes four), usually free; petals soon falling. Fruits are capsules. *Example* Purging flax *Linum catharticum*.

Ready reference – Flowering plant families vii

25 Geraniaceae Cranesbill family
Relatively large family of herbs, many of which are grown in the flower border or greenhouse (e.g. geraniums). *Leaves* forming a large clump or arranged alternately on the stems; palmately lobed or divided. *Flowers* wide open, solitary or in pairs or clusters on branched flower stalks; sepals and petals five, free, soon falling; stamens ten or fifteen, their bases fused together. Fruits are distinctive beaked capsules. *Example* Common storksbill *Erodium cicutarium*. See 24, 96 & p. 17(5).

26 Oxalidaceae Wood-sorrel family
Relatively large family of herbs. *Leaves* forming a clump or arranged alternately on the stems; compound or palmately lobed with three to many leaflets, often showing sleep movements. *Flowers* wide open, solitary or in small clusters; sepals and petals five, free; stamens ten. Fruits are capsules. *Example* Upright yellow sorrel *Oxalis europaea*. See 4.

28 Umbelliferae Carrot family
Large family of herbs and shrubs; several are grown as vegetables (e.g. parsnips) or herbs (e.g. parsley). Some are very poisonous (e.g. hemlock). *Leaves* usually finely divided forming a basl rosette or arranged alternately on the stems. Stems often grooved and/or hollow. *Flowers* in characteristic umbels; small and oftne star-like with five sepals united into a tube and five free petals. Fruits paired, each pair suspended from a central column. *Example* Hogweed *Heracleum sphondylium*. See 12, 19, 20, 90.

27 Malvaceae Mallow family
Relatively large family of trees, shrubs and herbs, some of which are economically important (e.g. cotton) or grown in flower borders (e.g. hollyhocks). *Leaves* often large and palmate, spirally arranged on the stems. *Flowers* wide open, solitary or in large spikes, often large and showy; sepals three to five, free or united; petals five, free. Fruits are capsules or a distinctive ring of fruits – a 'cheese'. *Example* Marsh mallow *Althaea officinalis*. See 99.

Ready reference – Flowering plant families viii

29 Crassulaceae Stonecrop family
Large family of herbs, often succulent and associated with warm dry habitats. *Leaves* simple, often succulent, growing in dense rosettes or variously arranged on the stems. *Flowers* often star-like, in clusters or spikes; sepals and petals five, free or united into tubes depending on genus. Fruits are capsules or a cluster of pods. *Example* White stonecrop *Sedum album*. See 31, 34, 117 & p. 16.

30 Polygonaceae Dock family
Relatively large family of herbs, shrubs and climbers, several of which are serious weeds (e.g. docks), and others are grown in the garden (e.g. rhubarb). *Leaves* often with distinctive sheath-like membranous stipules; usually arranged alternately on the stems. *Flowers* usually small and often clustered into large flowering shoots; three to six sepals present, either green or petal-like, free or united into a tube; petals absent. Fruits small one-seeded nuts. *Example* Broad-leaved dock *Rumex obtusifolius*. See 40, 70, 82, 98, 119.

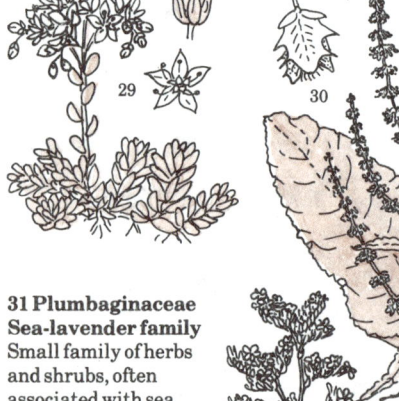

31 Plumbaginaceae Sea-lavender family
Small family of herbs and shrubs, often associated with sea shores. Some species are grown in the flower garden (e.g. statice). *Leaves* simple, often forming a basal rosette or arranged spirally on the stems. *Flowers* often enclosed in papery bracts; clustered into heads or loose spikes; five membranous sepals are united into a tube and five petals are free or joined at the base. Fruits are thin and papery. *Example* Rock sea-lavender *Limonium binervosum*. See 121.

32 Ericaceae Heather family
Large family of shrubs and trees, often associated with acid soils; many are grown in the shrub border (e.g. rhododendrons). *Leaves* simple, opposite or alternately arranged on the stems. *Flowers* waxy in appearance, often bell-shaped or funnel-shaped; sepals and petals three to seven (often five); sepals small, petals usually joined into a tube, sometimes free. Fruits are capsules or berries. *Example* Cowberry *Vaccinium vitis-idaea*. See 103, 104, 106, 107, 120.

Ready reference – Flowering plant families ix

33 Boraginaceae Borage family
Large family of herbs, rarely shrubs, many grown in the flower garden (e.g. anchusas). *Leaves* simple sometimes large, usually alternately arranged on the stems; leaves and stems often coarsely hairy. *Flowers* often bell-shaped or funnel-shaped, arranged in distinctive one-sided curled clusters; sepals and petals five, joined into tubes. Fruit is formed of four nutlets. *Example* Alkanet *Pentagtottis sempervirens*. See 52, 64.

34 Campanulaceae Bellflower family
Relatively large family of herbs, many grown in flower borders and rock gardens (e.g. Canterbury bells). *Leaves* usually simple, arranged alternately on the stems. Stems nearly always contain milky sap. *Flowers* bell-shaped, solitary or in spikes or clusters; five sepals and petals, united into tubes. Stamens as many as petals and alternating with them. Fruits usually capsules. *Example* Large bellflower *Campanula latifolia*. See 111.

35 Primulaceae Primrose family
Small family of herbs, several of which are grown in the flower garden (e.g. polyanthus, cyclamen). *Leaves* simple or divided, often in basal rosettes or arranged in whorls on the stems. *Flowers* solitary or in whorled spikes; wide open or funnel-shaped, usually with five (may be four to nine) sepals and petals, united into tubes (sometimes petals absent). Fruits are capsules. *Example* Yellow pimpernel *Lysimachia nemorum*. See 16, 42, 77.

36 Gentianaceae Gentian family
Relatively large family of herbs, several of which are grown in flower and rock gardens (e.g. gentians). *Leaves* simple, arranged in opposite pairs on the stems, often without stalks. *Flowers* in leafy clusters; often funnel-shaped with four or five sepals and petals, both united into tubes. Stamens as many as and alternating with the petals. Fruits are capsules with many tiny seeds. *Example* Common centaury *Centaurium erythraea*.

28 Ready reference – Flowering plant families x

37 Convolvulaceae Bindweed family
Relatively large family of herbs and climbing plants. *Leaves* simple, alternately arranged on the stems. Stems often contain milky juice. *Flowers* solitary or in small sprays, funnel-shaped or bell-shaped with bracts beneath the sepals; five free or united sepals and five united petals. Fruits are capsules. *Example* Bindweed *Convolvulus arvensis*. See 102.

38 Solanaceae Nightshade family
Large family of herbs and shrubs, many of economic importance (e.g. potato, tobacco). All are poisonous, many deadly (e.g. belladonna). *Leaves* simple, alternately arranged on the stems.
Flowers solitary or in small clusters in leaf axils; five fused anthers form the centre of the flower – a distinctive feature. Sepals and petals five, partially united into tubes. Fruits are capsules or berries. *Example* Henbane *Hyoscyamus niger*. See 100.

39 Scrophulariaceae Figwort family
Large family of herbs and shrubs, many of which are grown in flower borders (e.g. penstemons, antirrhinums).
Leaves simple, sometimes toothed, often in a basal rosette or variously arranged on the stems.
Flowers solitary or in terminal clusters or spikes or in leaf axils; two-lipped or funnel-shaped with four or five fused sepals and petals, both joined into tubes. Fruits are capsules. *Example* Figwort *Scrophularia nodosa*. See 7, 30, 32, 54, 62, 65, 88, 112.

40 Labiatae Mint family
Very large family of herbs and shrubs, many grown as culinary herbs (e.g. mint, thyme) or in flower borders (e.g. salvias). *Leaves* simple, in opposite pairs on quadrangular stems; often scented. *Flowers* usually in whorls in leaf axils; sepals form a five-toothed tube; petals five, fused to form a one- or two-lipped tubular flower. Fruits formed of four nutlets. *Example* Self-heal *Prunella vulgaris*. See 10, 17, 43, 66.

Ready reference – Flowering plant families xi

41 Rubiaceae Bedstraw family

Very large family of herbs and shrubs. *Leaves* simple, with stipules; arranged in opposite pairs or in whorls of leaves and leaf-like stipules on the stems.
Flowers small, funnel-shaped, usually in clusters or heads, terminal or in leaf axils; sepals and petals four to six; sepals free, petals joined into a tube. Fruits are capsules or small and one-seeded. *Example* Field madder *Sherardia arvensis*. *See* 23, 47, 113 & p. 17 (2).

42 Valerianaceae Valerian family

Small family of herbs, sometimes rather woody, with scented underground stems. *Leaves* simple or divided, in basal rosettes or in opposite pairs on the stems. *Flowers* small, funnel-shaped, in dense heads of many flowers; sepals form a toothed tube and often persist as a feathery cap on the small dry fruits; petals three to five, united into a tube. *Example* Valerian *Valeriana officinalis*. *See* 33.

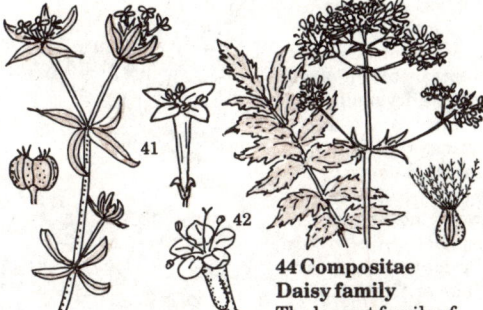

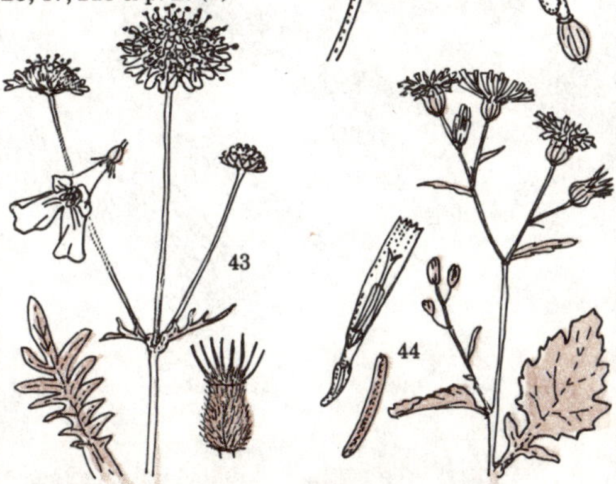

44 Compositae Daisy family

The largest family of flowering plants, many of economic importance (e.g. sunflowers) or grown in gardens (e.g. asters) or weeds (e.g. coltsfoot).
Leaves very varied.
Flowers distinctive, in heads which are often mistaken for individual flowers. In fact, each 'flower' consists of many tubular flowers (disc florets) and/or strap-shaped flowers (ray florets). Fruits are dry and one-seeded, often hairy.
Example Nipplewort *Lapsana communis*. *See* 25, 26, 27, 29, 37, 48, 60, 75, 80, 85, 86, 91, 92, 93, 101, 114 & p. 17 (7).

43 Dipsacacaea Scabious family

Very small family of herbs. *Leaves* simple or divided, in opposite pairs or in whorls on the stems. *Flowers* small, in large, many-flowered heads; sepals and petals four or five; sepals small, joined to form a cup; petals joined into a tube which may be two-lipped. Fruits dry and one-seeded. *Example* Field scabious *Knautia arvensis*. *See* 51.

30 Woodland

The number and kind of flowers found in a wood depend on the density and type of trees present. Trees like pine or spruce cast such deep, year-round shade that little grows beneath. Wild flowers that grow in deciduous woods often flower in spring and die down in summer when the dense leaf canopy cuts down light and water is drawn from the soil. Oak, ash and beech woods all have characteristic floras which also vary with soil acidity.

1 Wood anemone
Anemone nemorosa
Creeping underground stems enable the plant to survive dry summers and cold winters. In spring, white flowers appear, followed by palmate leaves which carpet the ground, especially in oak woods. The plant dies down in summer. Grows to 15 cm high.

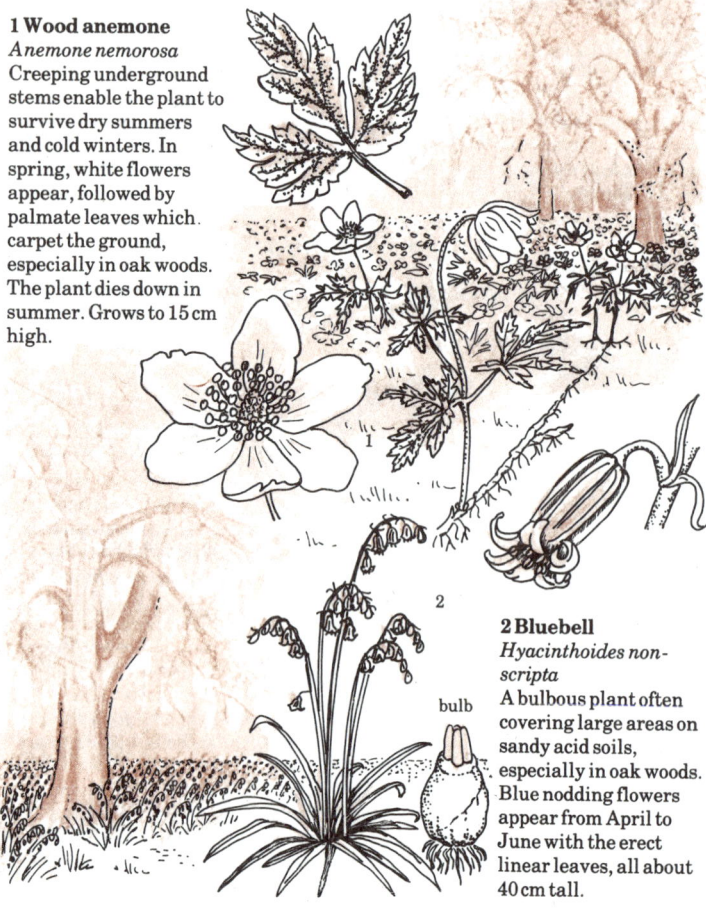

2 Bluebell
Hyacinthoides non-scripta
A bulbous plant often covering large areas on sandy acid soils, especially in oak woods. Blue nodding flowers appear from April to June with the erect linear leaves, all about 40 cm tall.

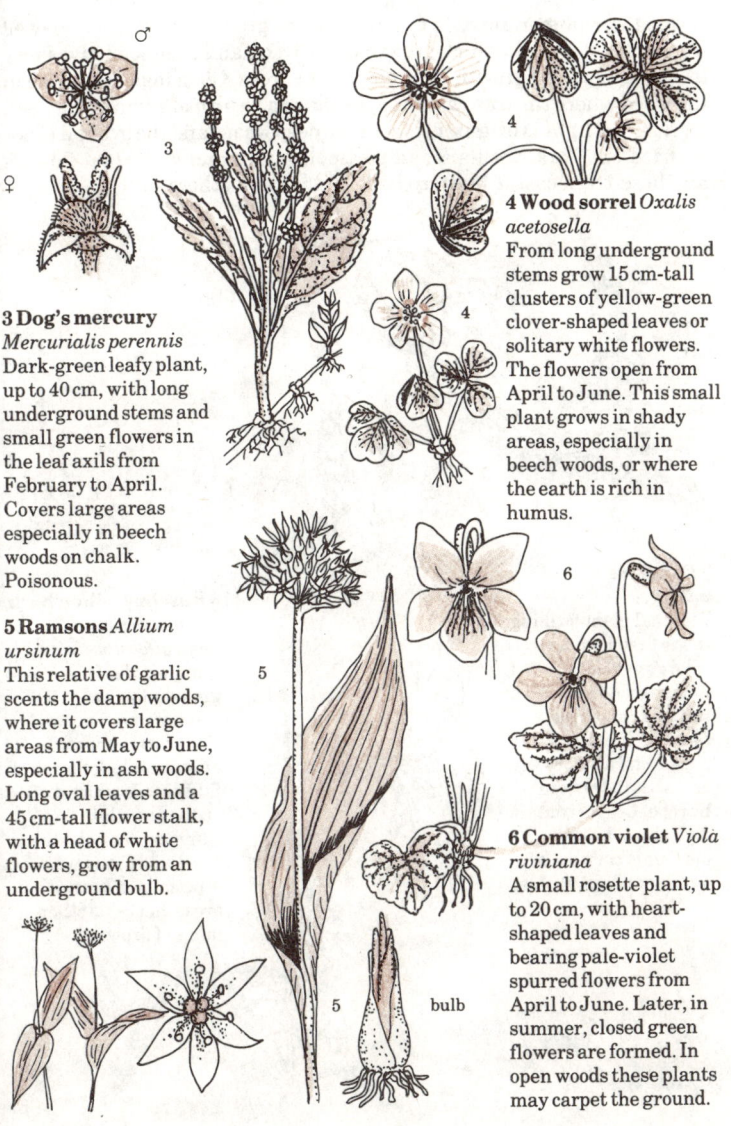

3 Dog's mercury
Mercurialis perennis
Dark-green leafy plant, up to 40 cm, with long underground stems and small green flowers in the leaf axils from February to April. Covers large areas especially in beech woods on chalk. Poisonous.

5 Ramsons *Allium ursinum*
This relative of garlic scents the damp woods, where it covers large areas from May to June, especially in ash woods. Long oval leaves and a 45 cm-tall flower stalk, with a head of white flowers, grow from an underground bulb.

4 Wood sorrel *Oxalis acetosella*
From long underground stems grow 15 cm-tall clusters of yellow-green clover-shaped leaves or solitary white flowers. The flowers open from April to June. This small plant grows in shady areas, especially in beech woods, or where the earth is rich in humus.

6 Common violet *Viola riviniana*
A small rosette plant, up to 20 cm, with heart-shaped leaves and bearing pale-violet spurred flowers from April to June. Later, in summer, closed green flowers are formed. In open woods these plants may carpet the ground.

32 Woodland clearings

A wood in summer appears to have a dense ground cover when viewed from outside. But the thick growth of the woodland edge soon gives way to a much sparser growth deep among the trees. Clearings and areas in the wood where the trees are far apart have a wealth of summer flowers, for here the light is brighter than in the deep woods and the ground is not so dried out. Oak woodlands in particular have many summer flowers for these trees cast a lighter shade than many others.

7 Foxglove *Digitalis purpurea*
Biennial plant forming, in the first year, a rosette of large oval leaves and, in the second year, a 1 m-tall spike of purple flowers. The flowers appear in July. Grows on acid soils in western Europe. Leaves contain digitalin, a heart medicine, poisonous in quite small quantities.

8 Rosebay willowherb *Chamaenerion angustifolium*
Perennial leaf rosette grows into a 1 m-tall spike of rosy flowers. The flowers appear in July, and are followed by fluffy seeds which drift on the air in late summer. Wasteland and woodland clearings, especially in burned areas, hence its other name of fireweed.

seed

33

9 Perforate St. John's wort *Hypericum perforatum*
From a creeping stem grow tall branched flowering stalks up to 90 cm. Bright-yellow flowers with fluffy centres are at their best in July and August. A plant of neutral or calcareous soils, especially in oakwoods.

10 Bugle *Ajuga reptans*
Creeping stems bear at intervals rooted rosettes of oblong leaves. From these grow 30 cm-tall leafy flowering stalks with crowded terminal spikes of lipped blue flowers from May to July. Damp woods and meadows.

11 Wild strawberry *Fragaria vesca*
Long slender runners with small, rooted clumps of leaves, up to 30 cm tall, and white flowers in April to June, followed by small edible strawberries. Grassy spots in woods and hedgerows, especially on basic soils.

12 Wild angelica *Angelica sylvestris*
From a rosette of large compound leaves grows a tall hollow purplish flowering stalk, up to 2 m. Many small white flowers in large terminal umbels appear from July to September. Damp woods and wet meadows.

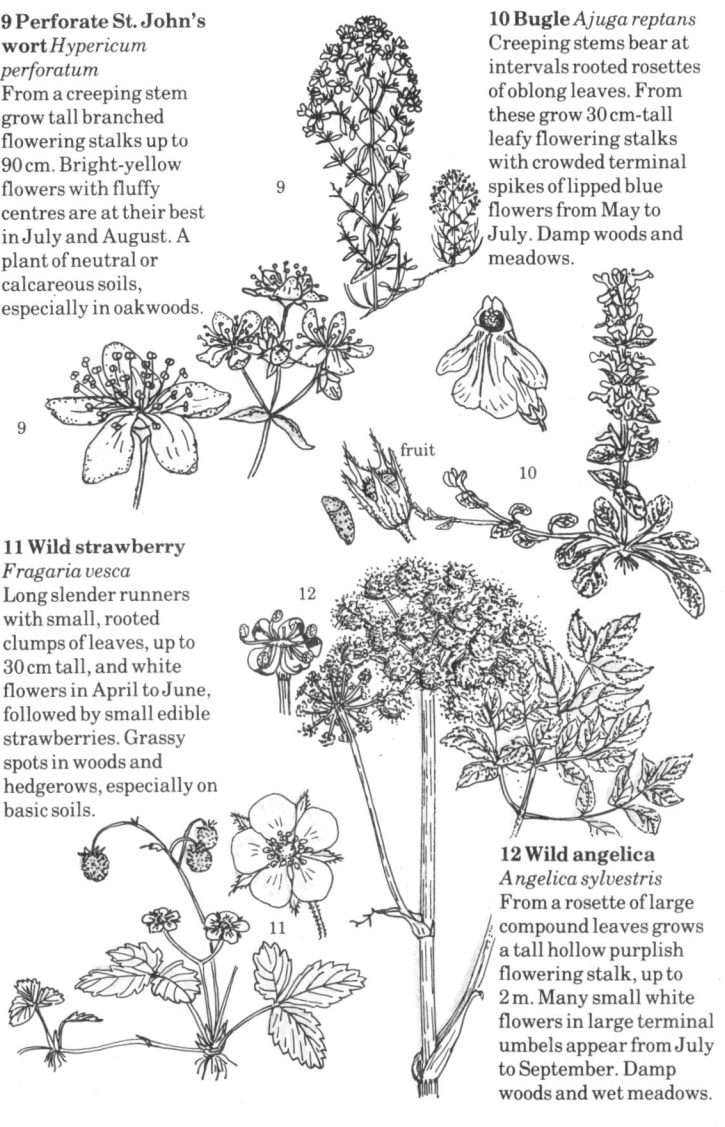

34 Hedgerows

Hedgerows are boundaries as far as people are concerned but are exactly the opposite to the plants and animals that live in them. To them they are living areas bounded by inhospitable open spaces. The hedges vary from narrow strips of clipped hawthorn or privet to wider bands with many species of trees and shrubs – almost a mini-woodland. The oldest hedgerows are of this wider type and are richest in plant species for they have been invaded over the years by woodland plants like those described below and opposite.

13 Greater stitchwort
Stellaria holostea
Forms a straggling clump of weak stems, up to 60 cm, with lance-shaped leaves and conspicuous white, satiny flowers in leaf axils in May and June. Hedgerows and woodland.

14 Red campion *Silene dioica*
Forms a spreading clump of erect flower stalks, up to 90 cm, with many large red-pink flowers in leaf axils, in May and June, followed by bladder-like seed capsules. Woodland edges and hedgerows, especially on basic soils.

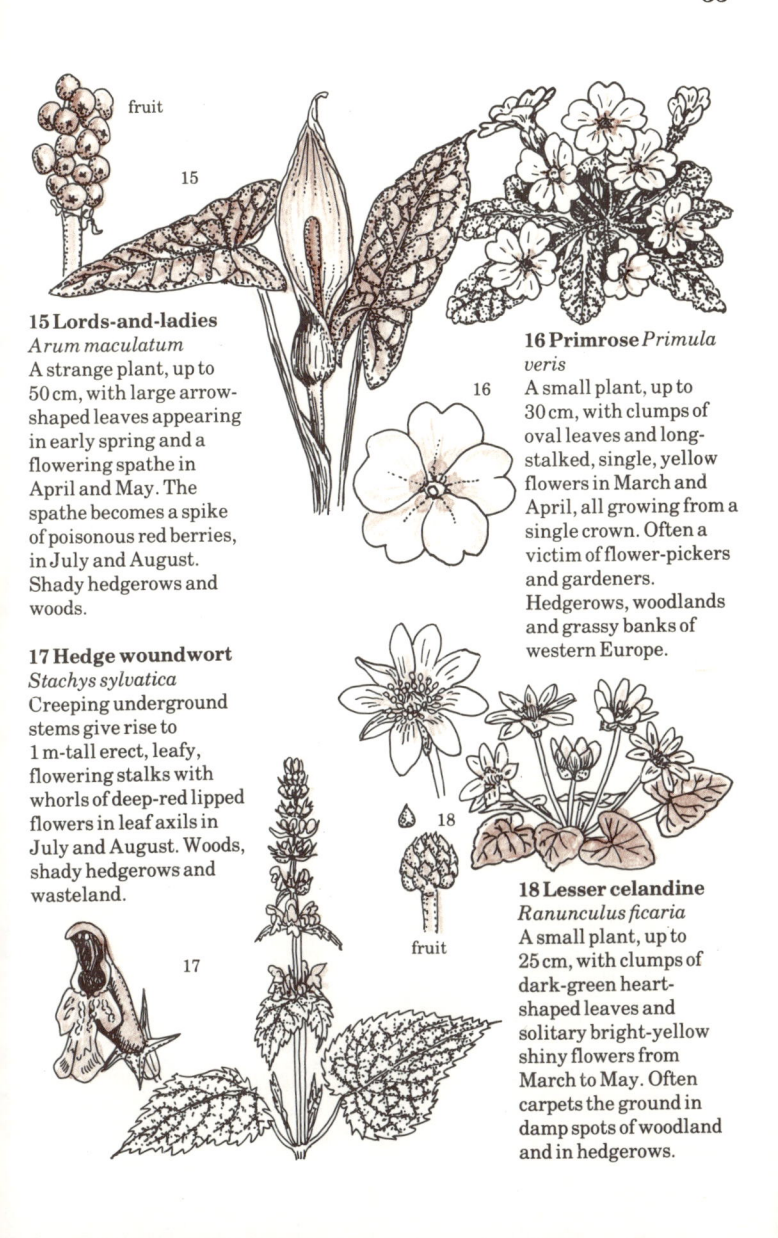

15 Lords-and-ladies
Arum maculatum
A strange plant, up to 50 cm, with large arrow-shaped leaves appearing in early spring and a flowering spathe in April and May. The spathe becomes a spike of poisonous red berries, in July and August. Shady hedgerows and woods.

16 Primrose *Primula veris*
A small plant, up to 30 cm, with clumps of oval leaves and long-stalked, single, yellow flowers in March and April, all growing from a single crown. Often a victim of flower-pickers and gardeners. Hedgerows, woodlands and grassy banks of western Europe.

17 Hedge woundwort
Stachys sylvatica
Creeping underground stems give rise to 1 m-tall erect, leafy, flowering stalks with whorls of deep-red lipped flowers in leaf axils in July and August. Woods, shady hedgerows and wasteland.

18 Lesser celandine
Ranunculus ficaria
A small plant, up to 25 cm, with clumps of dark-green heart-shaped leaves and solitary bright-yellow shiny flowers from March to May. Often carpets the ground in damp spots of woodland and in hedgerows.

36 Hedgebanks

Many farming areas have raised hedgebanks edging their fields, rather than woodland-type hedgerows. The hedgebanks often have steep grassy slopes which may or may not be topped by a narrow strip of hawthorn or similar shrub. Plants that grow well in sheltered grassland do well in this type of hedgerow. As many woodland hedges are being removed to increase field sizes, then narrow, almost flat, grassy hedgebanks are becoming more common. They tend to disappear under cow parsley plants in early summer.

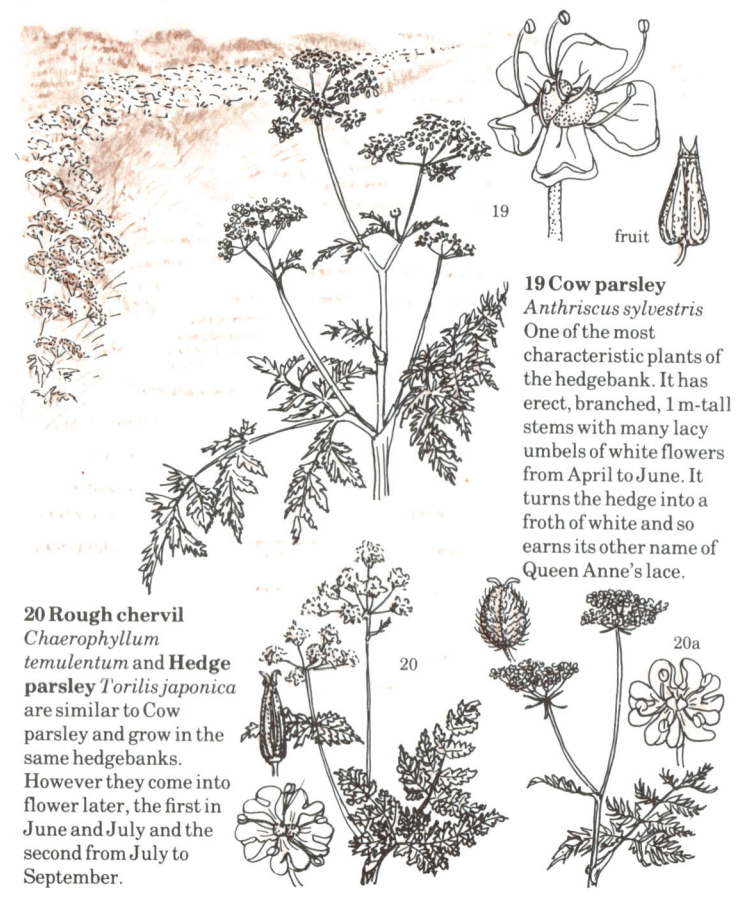

19 Cow parsley
Anthriscus sylvestris
One of the most characteristic plants of the hedgebank. It has erect, branched, 1 m-tall stems with many lacy umbels of white flowers from April to June. It turns the hedge into a froth of white and so earns its other name of Queen Anne's lace.

20 Rough chervil
Chaerophyllum temulentum and **Hedge parsley** *Torilis japonica* are similar to Cow parsley and grow in the same hedgebanks. However they come into flower later, the first in June and July and the second from July to September.

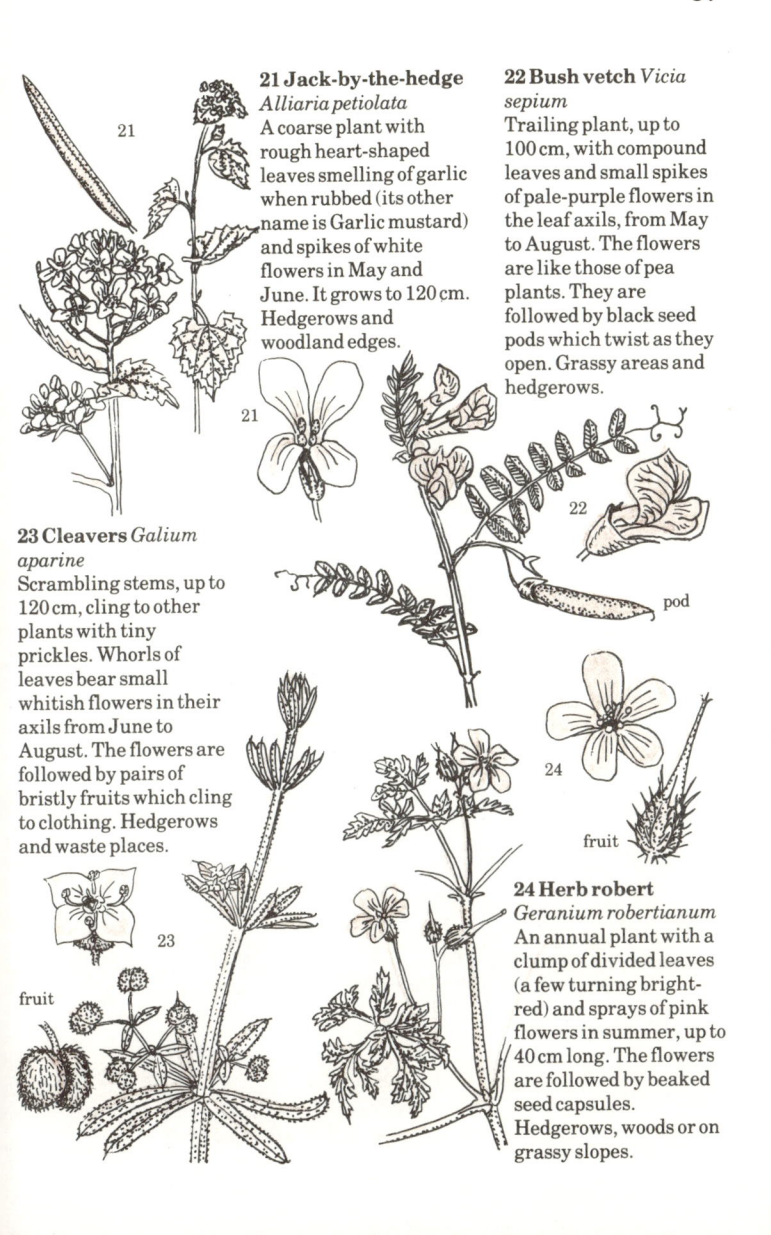

21 Jack-by-the-hedge
Alliaria petiolata
A coarse plant with rough heart-shaped leaves smelling of garlic when rubbed (its other name is Garlic mustard) and spikes of white flowers in May and June. It grows to 120 cm. Hedgerows and woodland edges.

22 Bush vetch *Vicia sepium*
Trailing plant, up to 100 cm, with compound leaves and small spikes of pale-purple flowers in the leaf axils, from May to August. The flowers are like those of pea plants. They are followed by black seed pods which twist as they open. Grassy areas and hedgerows.

pod

23 Cleavers *Galium aparine*
Scrambling stems, up to 120 cm, cling to other plants with tiny prickles. Whorls of leaves bear small whitish flowers in their axils from June to August. The flowers are followed by pairs of bristly fruits which cling to clothing. Hedgerows and waste places.

fruit

fruit

24 Herb robert
Geranium robertianum
An annual plant with a clump of divided leaves (a few turning bright-red) and sprays of pink flowers in summer, up to 40 cm long. The flowers are followed by beaked seed capsules. Hedgerows, woods or on grassy slopes.

38 Roadside verges

Grassy roadside verges are often dry inhospitable areas. They are open to burning sun and are trodden on by many feet. Only the toughest plants, like those included here, can survive. Many of them are able to limit water loss by having creeping stems with furry leaves that hug the ground or by having hairy or spiny stems. They all have deep, penetrating roots. Creeping stems are also well adapted to withstand trampling, and spiny plants are avoided even in highly populated areas.

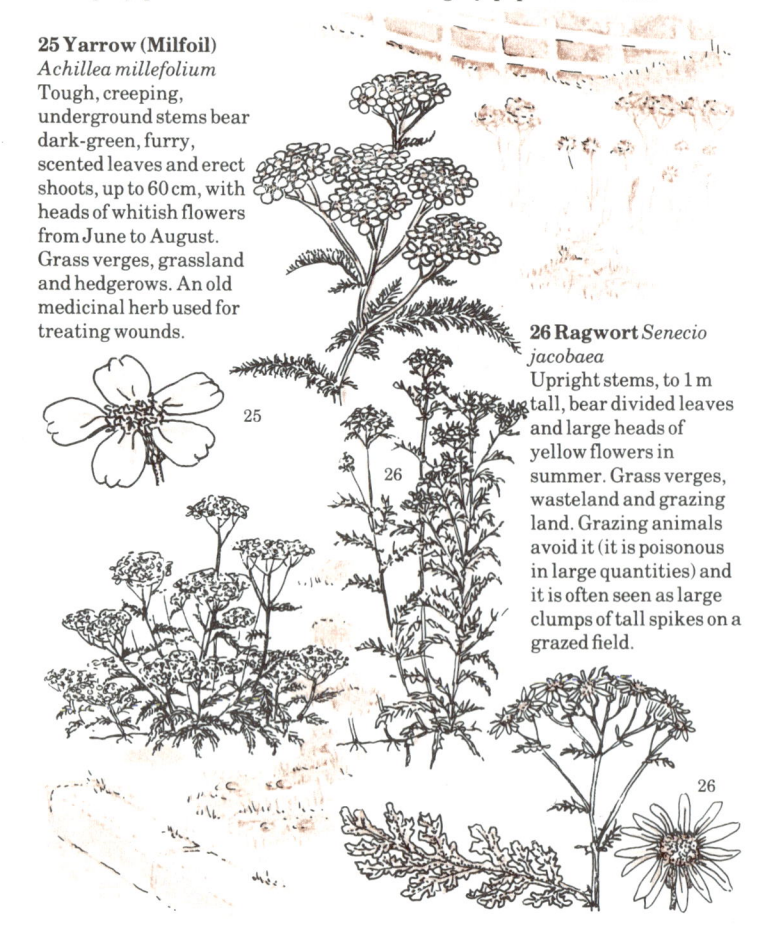

25 Yarrow (Milfoil)
Achillea millefolium
Tough, creeping, underground stems bear dark-green, furry, scented leaves and erect shoots, up to 60 cm, with heads of whitish flowers from June to August. Grass verges, grassland and hedgerows. An old medicinal herb used for treating wounds.

26 Ragwort *Senecio jacobaea*
Upright stems, to 1 m tall, bear divided leaves and large heads of yellow flowers in summer. Grass verges, wasteland and grazing land. Grazing animals avoid it (it is poisonous in large quantities) and it is often seen as large clumps of tall spikes on a grazed field.

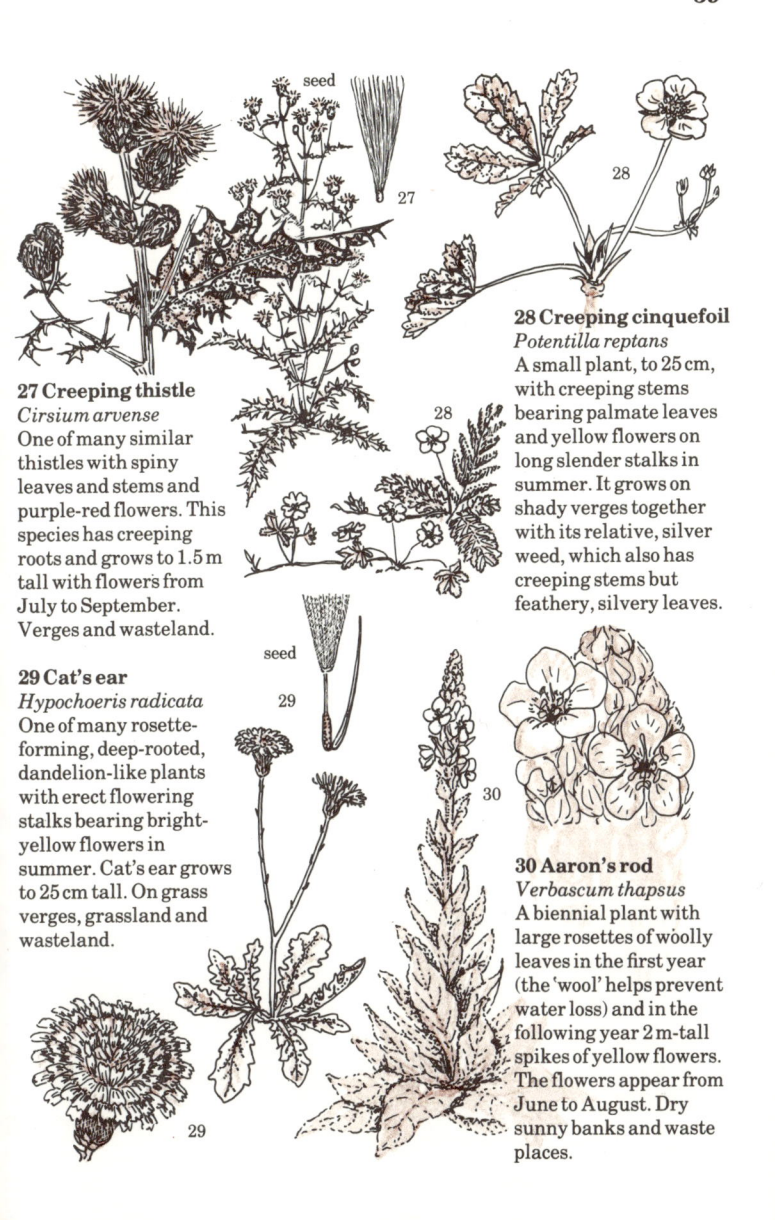

27 Creeping thistle
Cirsium arvense
One of many similar thistles with spiny leaves and stems and purple-red flowers. This species has creeping roots and grows to 1.5 m tall with flowers from July to September. Verges and wasteland.

28 Creeping cinquefoil
Potentilla reptans
A small plant, to 25 cm, with creeping stems bearing palmate leaves and yellow flowers on long slender stalks in summer. It grows on shady verges together with its relative, silver weed, which also has creeping stems but feathery, silvery leaves.

29 Cat's ear
Hypochoeris radicata
One of many rosette-forming, deep-rooted, dandelion-like plants with erect flowering stalks bearing bright-yellow flowers in summer. Cat's ear grows to 25 cm tall. On grass verges, grassland and wasteland.

30 Aaron's rod
Verbascum thapsus
A biennial plant with large rosettes of woolly leaves in the first year (the 'wool' helps prevent water loss) and in the following year 2 m-tall spikes of yellow flowers. The flowers appear from June to August. Dry sunny banks and waste places.

40 Walls

Whether they are the 'upland dry' or the 'village garden' type with crumbling mortar, walls provide a specialized habitat. They are usually made of limestone blocks that have many crevices in which plants can shelter. But walls form a dry environment; the plants that grow on them must be able to endure drought. A wall that faces north/south has a shady side and a sunny side, and the two aspects often present rather different appearances, with more mosses and ferns on the north side.

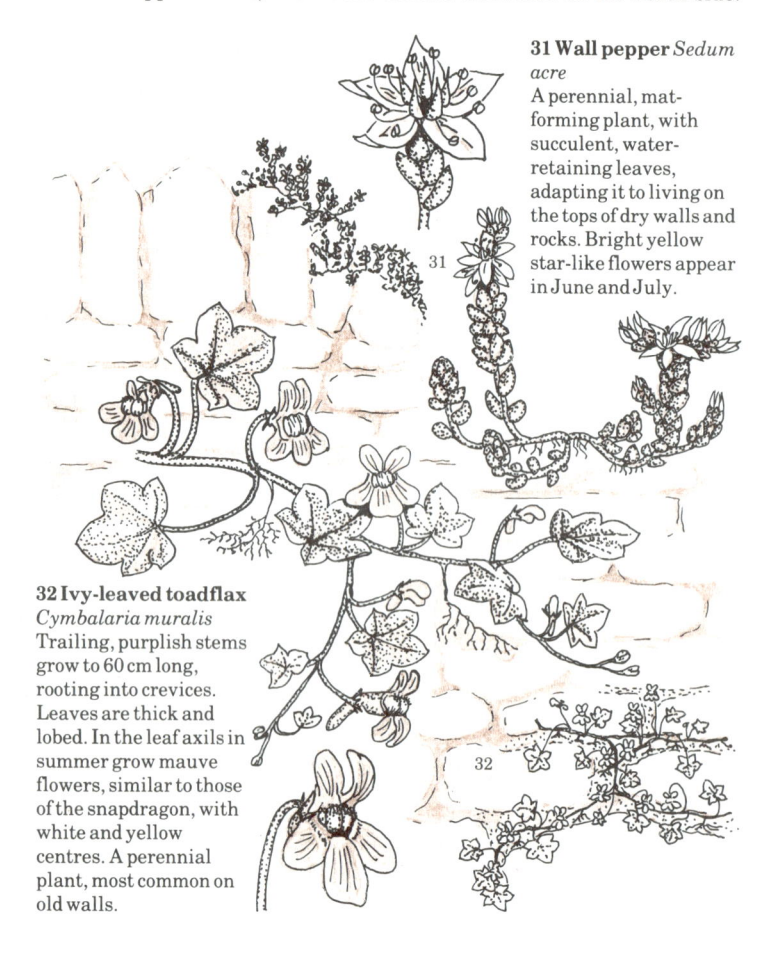

31 Wall pepper *Sedum acre*
A perennial, mat-forming plant, with succulent, water-retaining leaves, adapting it to living on the tops of dry walls and rocks. Bright yellow star-like flowers appear in June and July.

32 Ivy-leaved toadflax *Cymbalaria muralis*
Trailing, purplish stems grow to 60 cm long, rooting into crevices. Leaves are thick and lobed. In the leaf axils in summer grow mauve flowers, similar to those of the snapdragon, with white and yellow centres. A perennial plant, most common on old walls.

33 Red valerian
Centranthus ruber
Erect perennial plant with several stems to 80 cm, large leaves and heads of red, sweet-scented flowers in summer. Often seen on old village walls where its searching roots penetrate deep into the wall and can even displace the stones.

34 Wall pennywort
Umbilicus rupestris
Round succulent leaves form a perennial rosette from which grow erect flower stalks, up to 30 cm, with greenish, tubular flowers in summer. Shady crevices on the sides of old walls in western Europe in areas with high rainfall.

36 Yellow fumitory
Corydalis lutea
Forms a perennial clump to 30 cm high of smooth, divided leaves, with many sprays of spurred yellow flowers in summer. One of several garden plants which have escaped to grow wild on old village garden walls.

35 Whitlow grass
Erophila verna
An annual plant with small leaf rosettes in winter. Erect flower stalks, to 20 cm, grow in spring and bear white flowers from March to June. The seeds remain dormant through the hot summer on the wall and germinate in autumn.

fruit

42 Grasslands

Hayfields and grazing lands provide the most common large areas of grassland. Tall-growing wild flowers do well in hay fields providing they can flower and set seed before hay-making. Plants on grazing land are often lower-growing and so avoid damage by cattle or horses. Nowadays many fields have been ploughed and sown with special grasses and the wild flowers have mostly gone, but some old-fashioned fields survive. The latter contain a multitude of wild flowers, and other plants have found havens on grass verges.

37 Ox-eye daisy
Chrysanthemum leucanthemum
Erect flowering stalks, up to 70 cm, grow from perennial leaf rosettes in summer. Each stalk bears one or several daisies with white petals and a yellow centre; the flowers are at their best in May and June. All kinds of grassy places.

38 Meadow buttercup
Ranunculus acris
A perennial plant with branched erect stems, up to 80 cm, divided, deeply cut and toothed leaves, and many shiny yellow flowers from May to July. Damp areas in grassland in both lowlands and uplands. Avoided by cattle because of its acrid, burning taste.

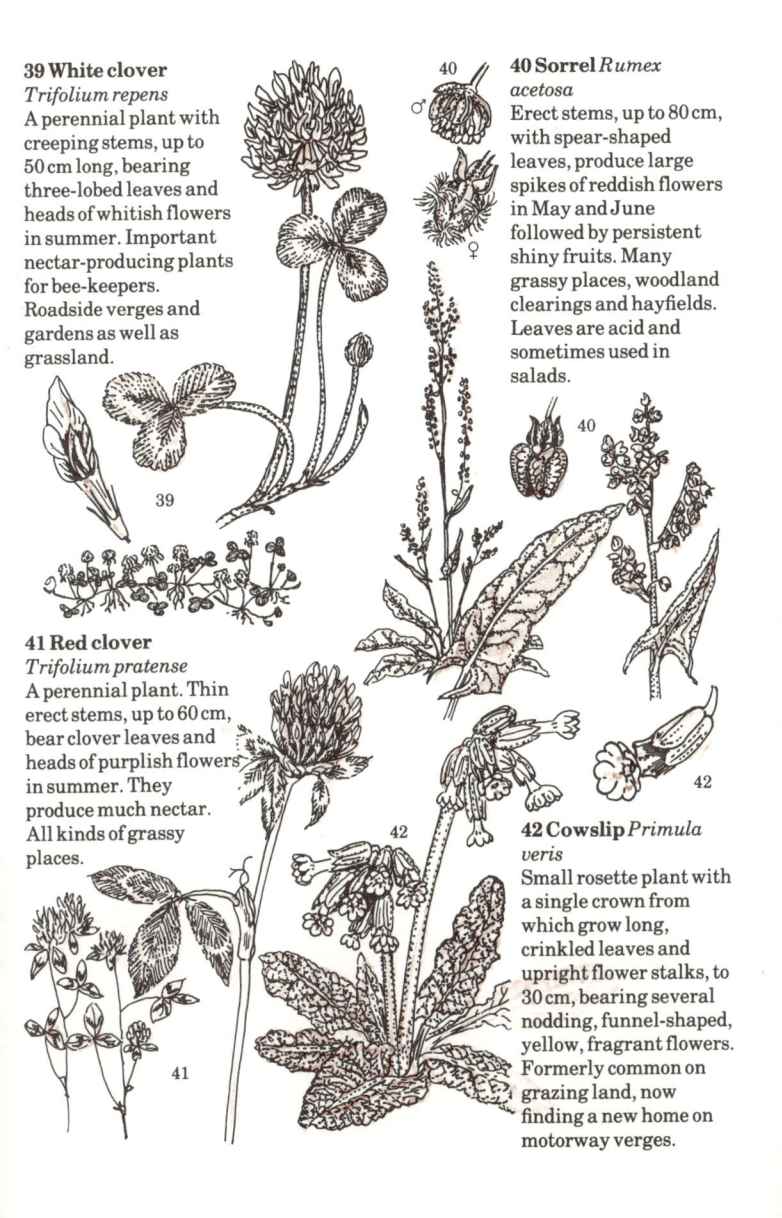

39 White clover
Trifolium repens
A perennial plant with creeping stems, up to 50 cm long, bearing three-lobed leaves and heads of whitish flowers in summer. Important nectar-producing plants for bee-keepers. Roadside verges and gardens as well as grassland.

40 Sorrel *Rumex acetosa*
Erect stems, up to 80 cm, with spear-shaped leaves, produce large spikes of reddish flowers in May and June followed by persistent shiny fruits. Many grassy places, woodland clearings and hayfields. Leaves are acid and sometimes used in salads.

41 Red clover
Trifolium pratense
A perennial plant. Thin erect stems, up to 60 cm, bear clover leaves and heads of purplish flowers in summer. They produce much nectar. All kinds of grassy places.

42 Cowslip *Primula veris*
Small rosette plant with a single crown from which grow long, crinkled leaves and upright flower stalks, to 30 cm, bearing several nodding, funnel-shaped, yellow, fragrant flowers. Formerly common on grazing land, now finding a new home on motorway verges.

44   Chalk and limestone downland

The old grassy, sheep-grazed downs and limestone uplands are covered by lime-loving wild flowers. The presence of sheep or rabbits is essential for maintaining the downs as the small, creeping or rosette-forming plants die out if the grazing stops. Then coarse grasses and scrubland trees invade the downs and the small plants cannot compete, soon stifled by lack of light and space. Many areas of downs have now been ploughed and are used for growing wheat and other cereals.

43 Thyme *Thymus drucei*
Tiny, mat-forming plant, rarely more than 5 cm high, with oval, scented leaves and heads of little purple flowers in summer. Only found in the shortest grassland and on rocky ground.

44 Common rockrose *Helianthemum chamaecistus*
Small shrub-like plant, up to 30 cm, with prostrate branches and small, narrow grey leaves. Flowers appear in leaf axils in summer, and are bright yellow. Each one lasts only for a day. Short grassland and rocky slopes.

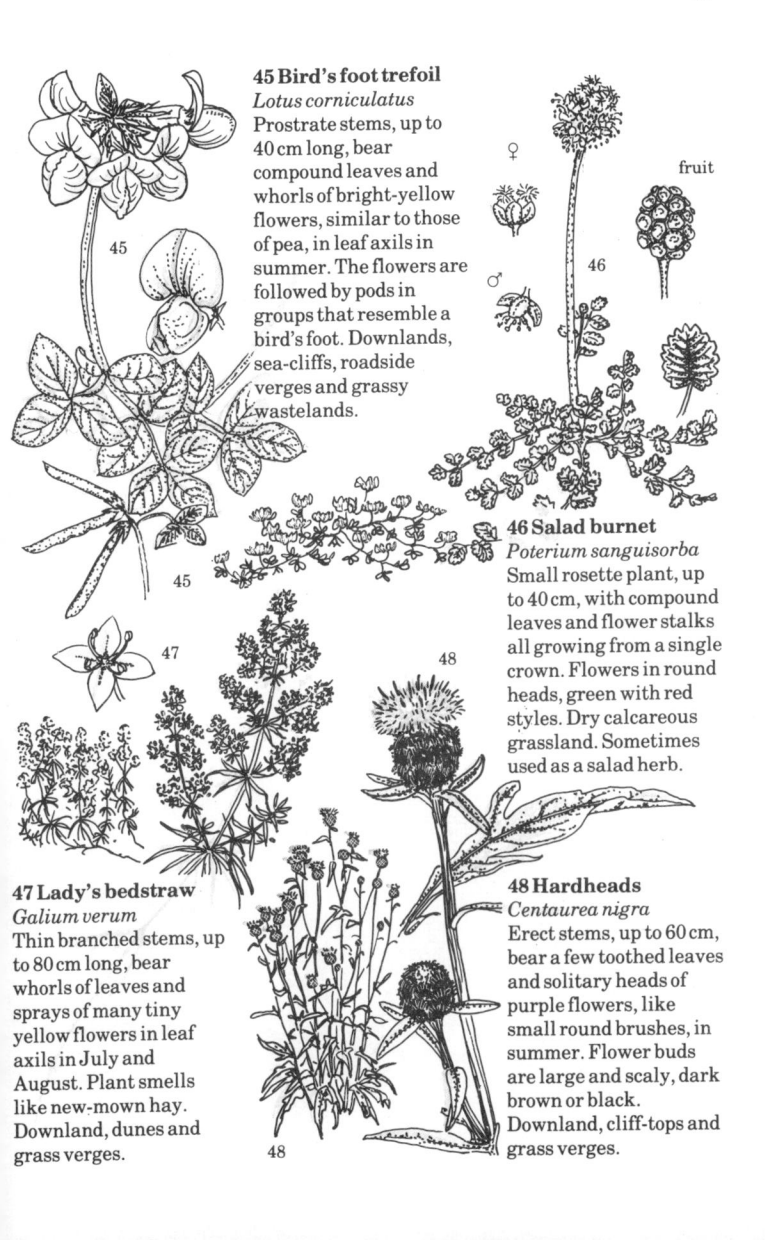

45 Bird's foot trefoil
Lotus corniculatus
Prostrate stems, up to 40 cm long, bear compound leaves and whorls of bright-yellow flowers, similar to those of pea, in leaf axils in summer. The flowers are followed by pods in groups that resemble a bird's foot. Downlands, sea-cliffs, roadside verges and grassy wastelands.

46 Salad burnet
Poterium sanguisorba
Small rosette plant, up to 40 cm, with compound leaves and flower stalks all growing from a single crown. Flowers in round heads, green with red styles. Dry calcareous grassland. Sometimes used as a salad herb.

47 Lady's bedstraw
Galium verum
Thin branched stems, up to 80 cm long, bear whorls of leaves and sprays of many tiny yellow flowers in leaf axils in July and August. Plant smells like new-mown hay. Downland, dunes and grass verges.

48 Hardheads
Centaurea nigra
Erect stems, up to 60 cm, bear a few toothed leaves and solitary heads of purple flowers, like small round brushes, in summer. Flower buds are large and scaly, dark brown or black. Downland, cliff-tops and grass verges.

46 Wet meadows and marshland

Wet meadows and marshes occur wherever the lie of the land results in the volume of water running into an area being greater than the volume lost through evaporation. They may be in upland valleys or low-lying flatlands, but always many wild flowers and insects live in them. Today, artificial drainage schemes have reduced the numbers of wet meadows and marshlands to the point where they are a fast-disappearing habitat. Conservation schemes are urgently needed to ensure the survival of at least some of them.

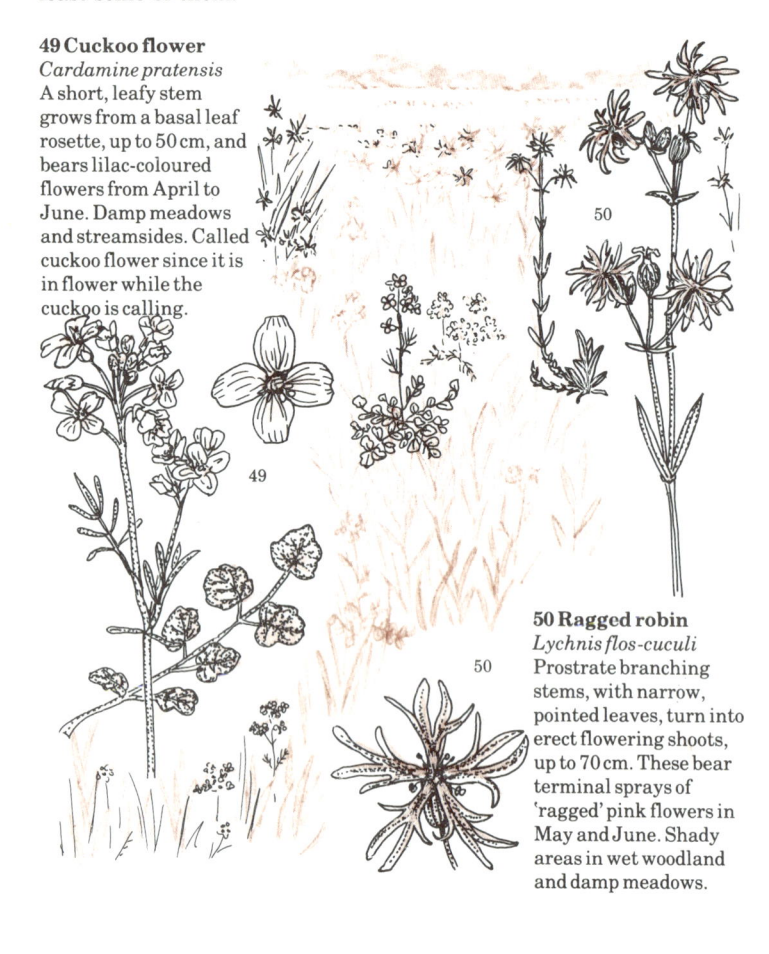

49 Cuckoo flower
Cardamine pratensis
A short, leafy stem grows from a basal leaf rosette, up to 50 cm, and bears lilac-coloured flowers from April to June. Damp meadows and streamsides. Called cuckoo flower since it is in flower while the cuckoo is calling.

50 Ragged robin
Lychnis flos-cuculi
Prostrate branching stems, with narrow, pointed leaves, turn into erect flowering shoots, up to 70 cm. These bear terminal sprays of 'ragged' pink flowers in May and June. Shady areas in wet woodland and damp meadows.

51 Devil's-bit scabious
Succisa pratensis
From a basal leaf rosette grows an erect flowering stem, to 30 cm. This has a few usually lance-shaped, stalkless leaves, and solitary heads of blue or purple flowers in summer. Damp meadows and woods, marshes and fens.

52 Comfrey
Symphytum officinale
A coarse leafy plant, to 1 m, with sprays of pink or white flowers in May and June. Marshlands and riversides. An old herbal plant used to treat wounds; another name for it is knitbone.

53 Spotted orchid
Dactylorhiza fuchsii
A variable species with a basal rosette of spear-shaped blotched leaves and an erect flowering stalk, up to 60 cm. This bears a head of pink or white flowers with red markings, from June to August. Marshes, wet meadows and dunes.

54 Lousewort
Pedicularis sylvatica
A small rosette of finely divided leaves gives rise to a short flowering stem, up to 25 cm, with pink flowers in May and June. These are followed by bladder-like seed capsules. A parasitic plant stunting the growth of surrounding plants. Wet ground.

48   Tall plants of the waterside

Water margins provide an ideal habitat for plants that like their roots in shallow water. Ditches, sloping edges of ponds or edges of unused canals are quickly colonized by such species. A pond is a temporary feature in a landscape compared to the land around, and it gradually silts up over hundreds of years. It is often possible to see a succession of different plants from deep water to the water's edge as the waterside plants colonize the pond, gradually creeping further towards the centre as the pond fills with mud.

55 Meadowsweet
Filipendula ulmaria
Rosettes of serrated leaves give rise to branched flower stalks, to 120 cm tall. Flowers are tiny, fluffy, creamy-white and scented and appear in terminal sprays in summer. A very common waterside plant, often in large colonies.

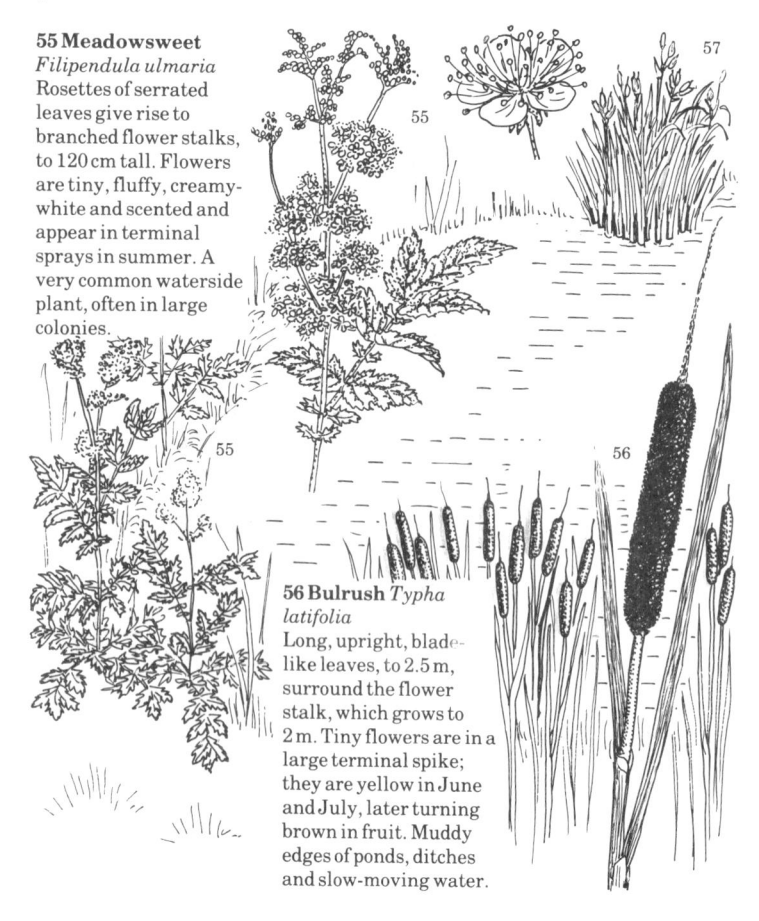

56 Bulrush *Typha latifolia*
Long, upright, blade-like leaves, to 2.5 m, surround the flower stalk, which grows to 2 m. Tiny flowers are in a large terminal spike; they are yellow in June and July, later turning brown in fruit. Muddy edges of ponds, ditches and slow-moving water.

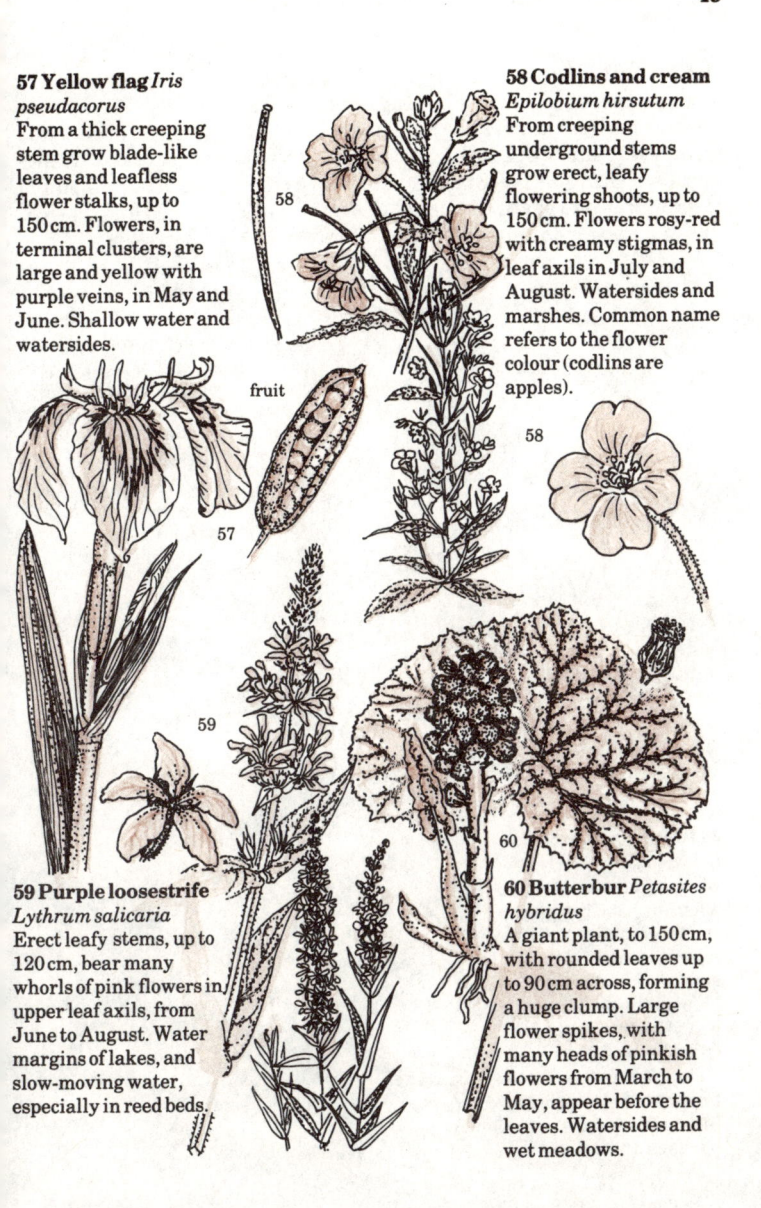

57 Yellow flag *Iris pseudacorus*
From a thick creeping stem grow blade-like leaves and leafless flower stalks, up to 150 cm. Flowers, in terminal clusters, are large and yellow with purple veins, in May and June. Shallow water and watersides.

58 Codlins and cream *Epilobium hirsutum*
From creeping underground stems grow erect, leafy flowering shoots, up to 150 cm. Flowers rosy-red with creamy stigmas, in leaf axils in July and August. Watersides and marshes. Common name refers to the flower colour (codlins are apples).

59 Purple loosestrife *Lythrum salicaria*
Erect leafy stems, up to 120 cm, bear many whorls of pink flowers in upper leaf axils, from June to August. Water margins of lakes, and slow-moving water, especially in reed beds.

60 Butterbur *Petasites hybridus*
A giant plant, to 150 cm, with rounded leaves up to 90 cm across, forming a huge clump. Large flower spikes, with many heads of pinkish flowers from March to May, appear before the leaves. Watersides and wet meadows.

50 Small plants of the waterside

Not all waterside plants are tall. Ponds and ditches are frequently dredged and in the year following dredging many smaller plants may colonize the open water. The banks of village or farm ponds are often too trampled to allow the tall water plants to thrive but the small plants may be able to survive. Streams often have too little mud for tall plants to grow and here again smaller plants may flourish, tucked into crevices in the banks or taking over backwaters.

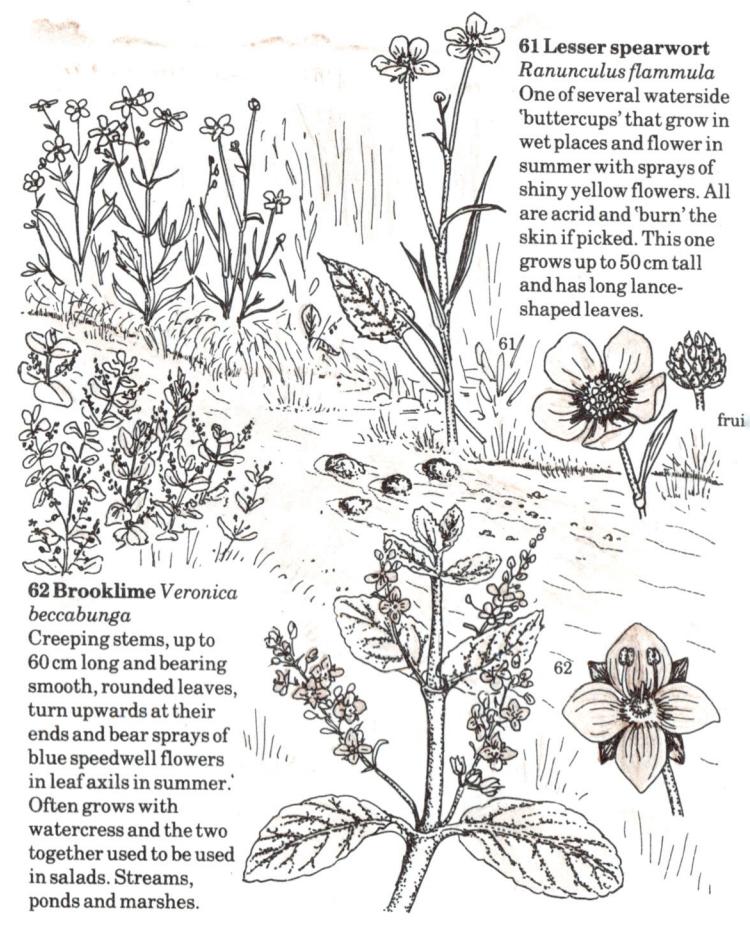

61 Lesser spearwort *Ranunculus flammula*
One of several waterside 'buttercups' that grow in wet places and flower in summer with sprays of shiny yellow flowers. All are acrid and 'burn' the skin if picked. This one grows up to 50 cm tall and has long lance-shaped leaves.

fruit

62 Brooklime *Veronica beccabunga*
Creeping stems, up to 60 cm long and bearing smooth, rounded leaves, turn upwards at their ends and bear sprays of blue speedwell flowers in leaf axils in summer. Often grows with watercress and the two together used to be used in salads. Streams, ponds and marshes.

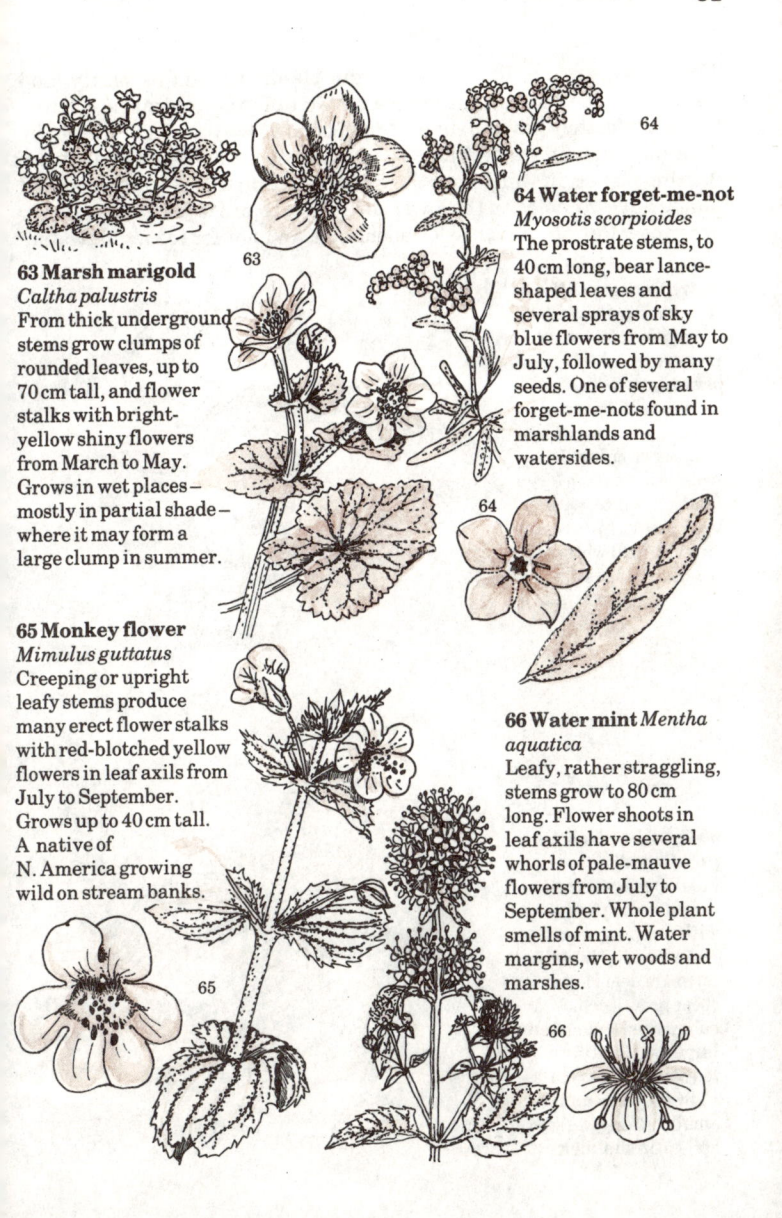

63 Marsh marigold
Caltha palustris
From thick underground stems grow clumps of rounded leaves, up to 70 cm tall, and flower stalks with bright-yellow shiny flowers from March to May. Grows in wet places — mostly in partial shade — where it may form a large clump in summer.

64 Water forget-me-not
Myosotis scorpioides
The prostrate stems, to 40 cm long, bear lance-shaped leaves and several sprays of sky blue flowers from May to July, followed by many seeds. One of several forget-me-nots found in marshlands and watersides.

65 Monkey flower
Mimulus guttatus
Creeping or upright leafy stems produce many erect flower stalks with red-blotched yellow flowers in leaf axils from July to September. Grows up to 40 cm tall. A native of N. America growing wild on stream banks.

66 Water mint *Mentha aquatica*
Leafy, rather straggling, stems grow to 80 cm long. Flower shoots in leaf axils have several whorls of pale-mauve flowers from July to September. Whole plant smells of mint. Water margins, wet woods and marshes.

52 Water plants

Water plants are unlike water-margin plants, which are mostly land plants that need extra water. They have a different internal structure; for example, they have no supporting tissues as they are kept upright by their buoyancy in water. Their leaves have no air holes unless they are floating leaves, in which case the air holes are on the top surface. (Land plants have air holes on the lower surfaces of their leaves.) Roots, if they are present at all, are only for anchorage and not for taking in water.

67 White water lily
Nymphaea alba
Clump-forming plant rooted in mud at bottom of water up to 3 m deep. Leaves with long stalks are the unmistakable floating circular 'lily pads'. Flowers are large, floating, white, with up to 25 petals, in July and August. Still water of ponds and lakes.

68 Broad-leaved pondweed
Potamogeton natans
One of many pondweeds with creeping stems rooted in mud in water up to 1 m deep. From these grow linear submerged leaves and large oval floating leaves with long stalks. Flowers green and small, on long-stalked spikes, in summer.

69 Duckweed *Lemna minor*

Small, floating, round leaves, often in threes, each with a single submerged root. Flowers tiny, on the surface of the leaves in June and July. Forms a green film on stagnant water in ponds and ditches.

70 Amphibious bistort *Polygonum amphibium*

Floating stems, up to 70 cm long, with floating oblong leaves and dense terminal flower spikes of many pink flowers from July to September. Ponds and slow-moving water or as a land form on the banks beside water.

71 Water crowfoot *Ranunculus aquatilis*

A small plant with submerged stems and two kinds of leaves. Floating leaves lobed, up to 5 cm across, submerged leaves finely divided. Flowers like white buttercups appear above the surface in May and June. Poisonous. Ponds and ditches.

72 Water plantain *Alisma plantago-aquatica*

Forms a clump of large arrow-shaped leaves and branched flower stalks, up to 80 cm long. Flowers white, open in the afternoon, from June to August. Rooted in the mud in shallow, slow-moving or still water.

54   Arable land

A variety of crops are grown on arable land, from wheat and barley to root crops and rapeseed. There are many species of wild flowers that grow in such fields, although they are neither so common nor so numerous as they were 30 years ago. This is mainly due to the use of weedkillers and improved methods of cleaning the crop seed before sowing so that the weed seeds are rejected. Most of the arable land wild plants now survive on field edges, roadside verges and waste places or they have all but died out.

73 Field poppy *Papaver rhoeas*
An annual plant with a bristly erect stem, up to 60 cm, and hairy leaves. Large red flowers grow in leaf axils from June to August, followed by seed capsules like pepper shakers. Edges of corn fields and waste places. Poisonous.

74 Charlock *Sinapis arvensis*
An annual plant with an erect, hairy, leafy stem, up to 80 cm, and many terminal sprays of bright-yellow flowers from May to July. Particularly on calcareous soils and was a serious weed of cornfields.

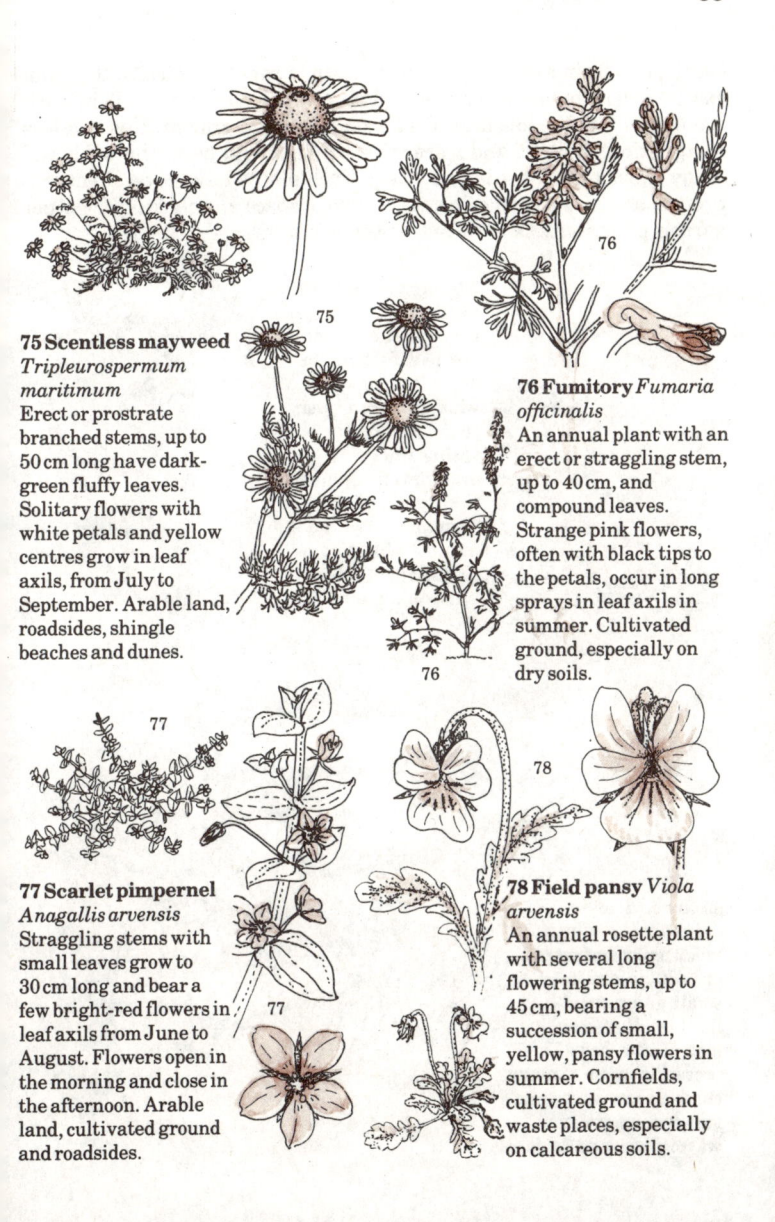

75 Scentless mayweed
Tripleurospermum maritimum
Erect or prostrate branched stems, up to 50 cm long have dark-green fluffy leaves. Solitary flowers with white petals and yellow centres grow in leaf axils, from July to September. Arable land, roadsides, shingle beaches and dunes.

76 Fumitory *Fumaria officinalis*
An annual plant with an erect or straggling stem, up to 40 cm, and compound leaves. Strange pink flowers, often with black tips to the petals, occur in long sprays in leaf axils in summer. Cultivated ground, especially on dry soils.

77 Scarlet pimpernel *Anagallis arvensis*
Straggling stems with small leaves grow to 30 cm long and bear a few bright-red flowers in leaf axils from June to August. Flowers open in the morning and close in the afternoon. Arable land, cultivated ground and roadsides.

78 Field pansy *Viola arvensis*
An annual rosette plant with several long flowering stems, up to 45 cm, bearing a succession of small, yellow, pansy flowers in summer. Cornfields, cultivated ground and waste places, especially on calcareous soils.

56 Annual garden plants

Gardens contain areas of good, bare earth, a rare condition in the wild, except where man's influence is felt. Annual plants do well in such conditions for the soil is fertile, promoting fast growth; there is less competition for light and water than there would be in the wild; and many thousands of seeds can be set. Such plants have several generations in a year, soon covering every inch of space and choking the other garden plants unless removed by the gardener.

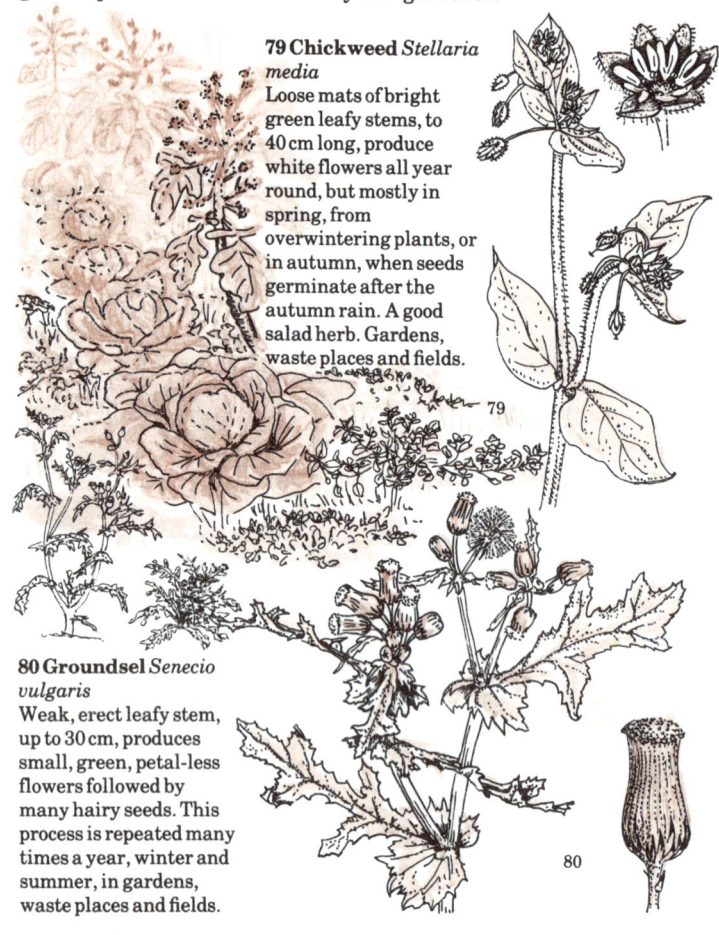

79 Chickweed *Stellaria media*
Loose mats of bright green leafy stems, to 40 cm long, produce white flowers all year round, but mostly in spring, from overwintering plants, or in autumn, when seeds germinate after the autumn rain. A good salad herb. Gardens, waste places and fields.

80 Groundsel *Senecio vulgaris*
Weak, erect leafy stem, up to 30 cm, produces small, green, petal-less flowers followed by many hairy seeds. This process is repeated many times a year, winter and summer, in gardens, waste places and fields.

81 Fat hen
Chenopodium album
Erect reddish stem, up to 1 m tall, has many large, deep-green, diamond- and lance-shaped leaves, and long spikes of green flowers from July to October, followed by many fatty seeds (giving the plant its name). Cultivated ground and farmyards.

82 Knotgrass
Polygonum aviculare
Variable species with prostrate or erect leafy stems, up to 2 m long, bearing dense spikes of pinkish flowers in leaf axils from July to October. Gardens, wasteland, arable land and seashores.

83 Sun spurge
Euphorbia helioscopia
Single stem, up to 40 cm tall, has bright-green leaves and terminal clusters of tiny green flowers, 'cupped' in green bracts, in summer. Stems full of milky juice that irritates the skin. Cultivated ground.

84 Shepherd's purse
Capsella bursa-pastoris
Small rosette plant with an erect flowering stalk, up to 30 cm tall, bearing many small white flowers, followed by purse-shaped seed capsules. Several generations a year. Cultivated ground and wasteland.

Perennial garden plants

To a gardener, perennial 'weeds' mean double trouble. Their seeds spread far and wide over the garden, while they often have deep underground roots or stems that can grow into a new plant if not completely removed. These plants are often highly successful in their competition with man. The battle over lawns is often most fierce for it is impossible to dig the weeds out without ruining the grass and perennial grassland plants find the short grass an ideal habitat.

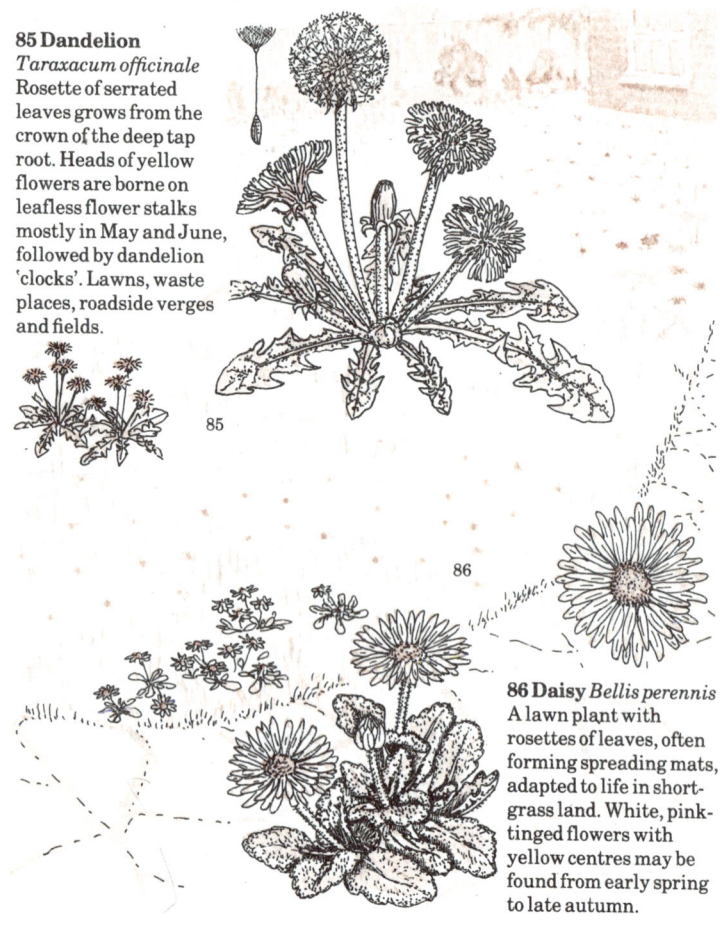

85 Dandelion
Taraxacum officinale
Rosette of serrated leaves grows from the crown of the deep tap root. Heads of yellow flowers are borne on leafless flower stalks mostly in May and June, followed by dandelion 'clocks'. Lawns, waste places, roadside verges and fields.

86 Daisy *Bellis perennis*
A lawn plant with rosettes of leaves, often forming spreading mats, adapted to life in short-grass land. White, pink-tinged flowers with yellow centres may be found from early spring to late autumn.

87 Ribwort *Plantago lanceolata*
Flat or erect rosette of long, ribbed leaves bears many leafless flower stalks with terminal heads of petal-less flowers which have conspicuous white stamens. All kinds of short-grass land, including lawns and roadside verges.

88 Germander speedwell *Veronica chamaedrys*
Prostrate leafy stems, up to 40 cm long, bear sprays of bright blue flowers in leaf axils from March to July. Shady areas of lawns, hedgerows and grassland.

89 Creeping buttercup *Ranunculus repens*
Creeping stems bear rooted rosettes of toothed 3-lobed leaves at intervals. From these grow erect flower stalks, up to 50 cm, with many shiny yellow flowers, from May to August. Damper areas of grassland, in lawns, wasteland and dunes.

90 Ground elder *Aegopodium podagraria*
One of the gardener's worst enemies. From creeping underground stems grow compound leaves (which can be cooked like spinach) and 1 m-tall flowering stalks with umbels of tiny whitish flowers from May to July. Gardens, hedges and wasteland.

60   Annual and biennial plants of wasteland

Wastelands are often temporary homes for plants – a building lot eventually becomes a new estate and waste ground a tarmac-covered car park. But in the meantime, annual and biennial plants that can complete their life cycles in one or two years respectively can take advantage of the open ground. Their seeds are borne on the wind or by birds or people (in dust in shoes) to germinate wherever there is a little soil or a crack in the concrete. These are the colonists of the plant world.

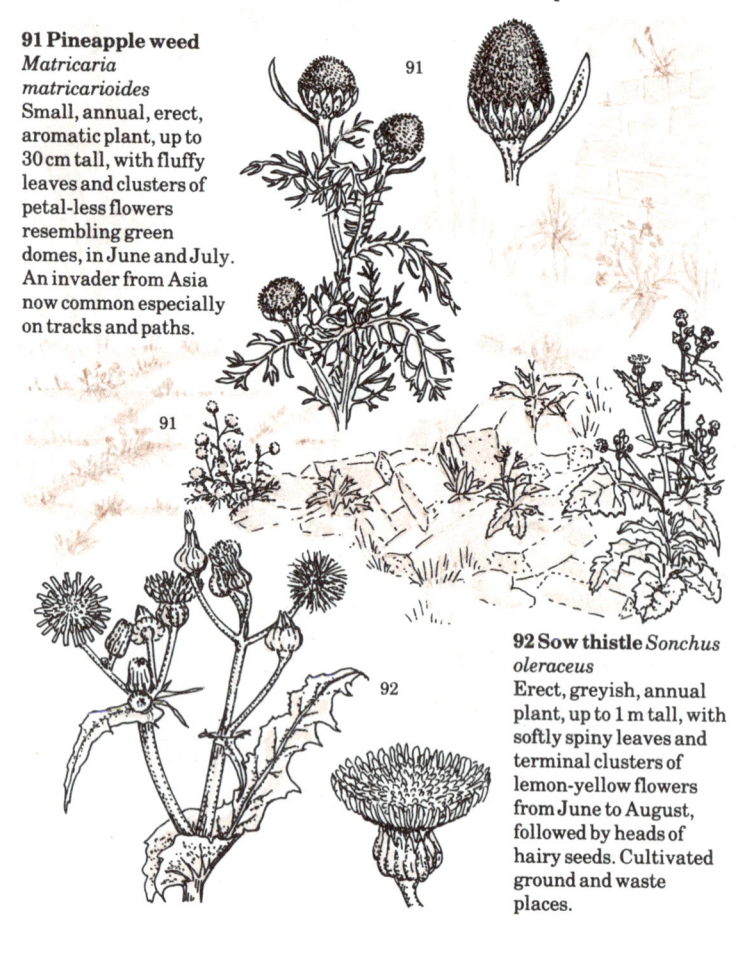

91 Pineapple weed *Matricaria matricarioides*
Small, annual, erect, aromatic plant, up to 30 cm tall, with fluffy leaves and clusters of petal-less flowers resembling green domes, in June and July. An invader from Asia now common especially on tracks and paths.

92 Sow thistle *Sonchus oleraceus*
Erect, greyish, annual plant, up to 1 m tall, with softly spiny leaves and terminal clusters of lemon-yellow flowers from June to August, followed by heads of hairy seeds. Cultivated ground and waste places.

61

93 Burdock *Arctium minus*
Clump of large overwintering leaves gives rise to an erect, branched, 1 m-tall flower stalk in July and August. Flowers reddish-purple in softly spiny heads, followed by scaly seeds – burrs – which cling to the clothing. Wasteland and woodland.

94 Policeman's helmet *Impatiens glandulifera*
A giant annual with erect, leafy, 2 m-tall stems and sprays of large helmet-shaped purple flowers in the upper leaf axils from July to October. Seed pods explosive. An Asian invader now rapidly colonising waste places and river banks.

95 Orache *Atriplex patula*
A variable plant with prostrate or erect leafy stems, up to 1 m long. Small, green, petal-less flowers are borne in sprays in upper leaf axils from July to September. Open places in wasteland and cultivated ground.

96 Cut-leaved cranesbill *Geranium dissectum*
Deeply divided leaves and branched straggling flower stalks, up to 40 cm long, grow from a single crown. Many small pink flowers in summer are followed by small beaked fruits. Wasteland and cultivated ground, grassy hedgerows.

62 Perennial wasteland plants

For townspeople, wastelands may present the best opportunity for seeing wild plants. There are always some of these areas in a city, places which have been forgotten by the planners, where plants and animals make their homes relatively undisturbed. A few such areas have become valuable nature reserves, oases in vast expanses of concrete and skyscrapers. Many of the plants living there are tough natives but occasionally foreign species may form small colonies, carried in by human visitors or in imported cargoes.

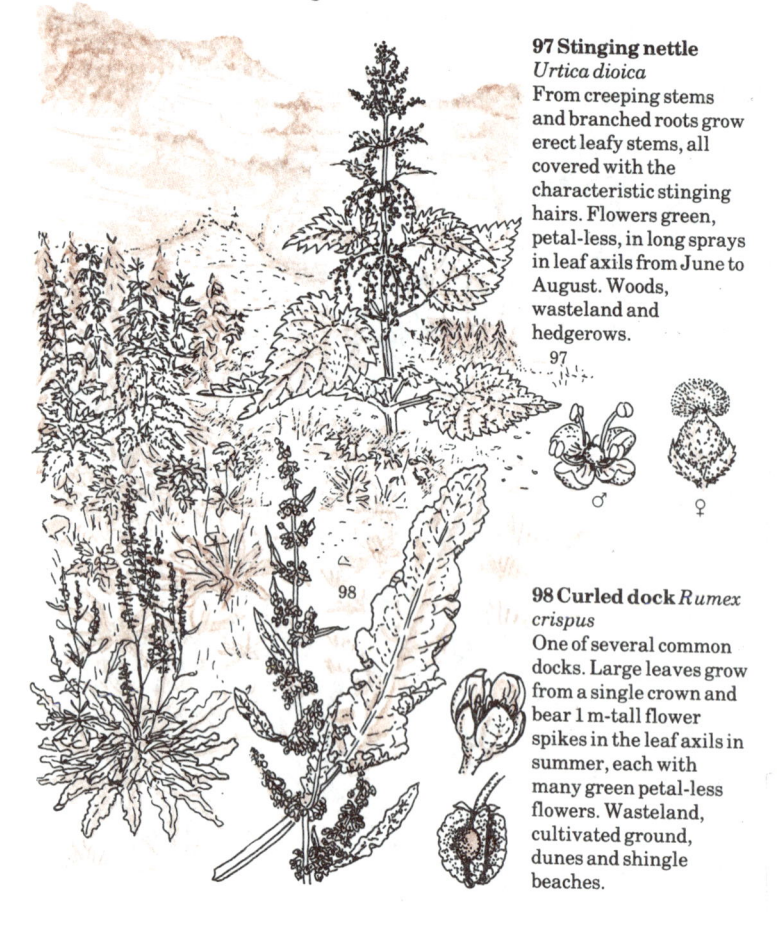

97 Stinging nettle
Urtica dioica
From creeping stems and branched roots grow erect leafy stems, all covered with the characteristic stinging hairs. Flowers green, petal-less, in long sprays in leaf axils from June to August. Woods, wasteland and hedgerows.

98 Curled dock *Rumex crispus*
One of several common docks. Large leaves grow from a single crown and bear 1 m-tall flower spikes in the leaf axils in summer, each with many green petal-less flowers. Wasteland, cultivated ground, dunes and shingle beaches.

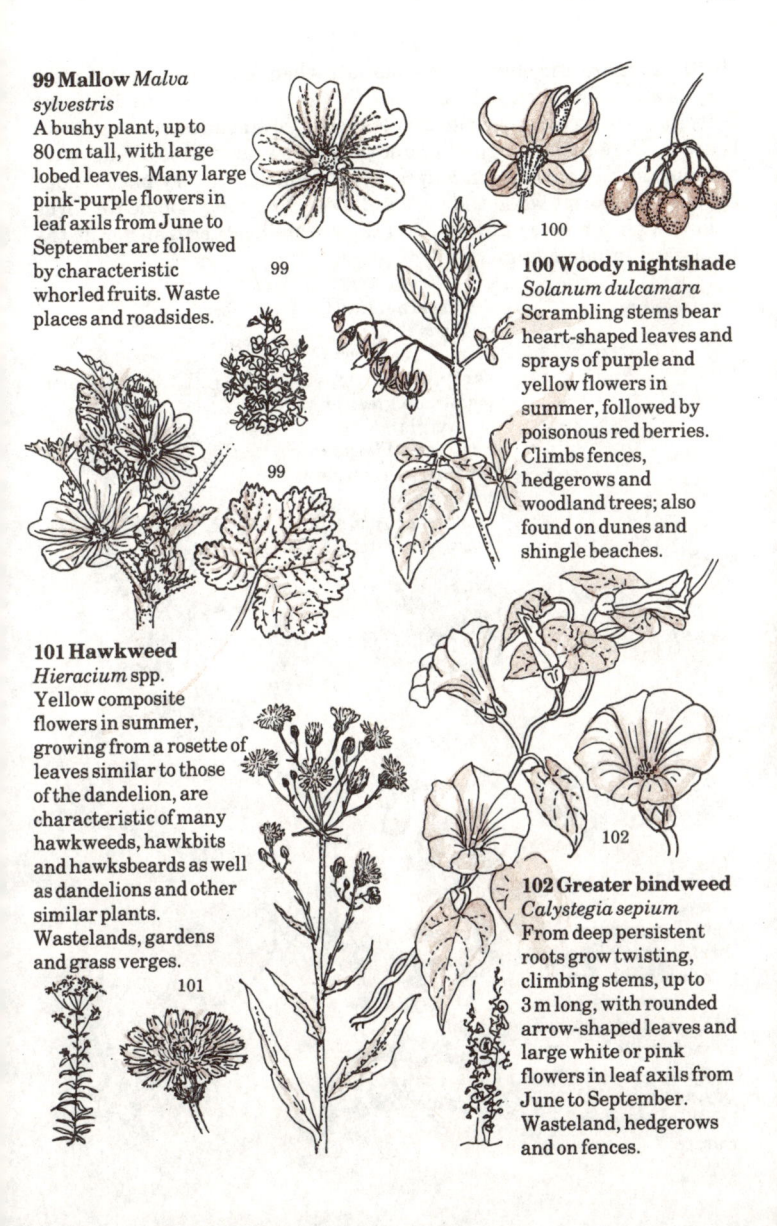

99 Mallow *Malva sylvestris*
A bushy plant, up to 80 cm tall, with large lobed leaves. Many large pink-purple flowers in leaf axils from June to September are followed by characteristic whorled fruits. Waste places and roadsides.

100 Woody nightshade *Solanum dulcamara*
Scrambling stems bear heart-shaped leaves and sprays of purple and yellow flowers in summer, followed by poisonous red berries. Climbs fences, hedgerows and woodland trees; also found on dunes and shingle beaches.

101 Hawkweed *Hieracium* spp.
Yellow composite flowers in summer, growing from a rosette of leaves similar to those of the dandelion, are characteristic of many hawkweeds, hawkbits and hawksbeards as well as dandelions and other similar plants. Wastelands, gardens and grass verges.

102 Greater bindweed *Calystegia sepium*
From deep persistent roots grow twisting, climbing stems, up to 3 m long, with rounded arrow-shaped leaves and large white or pink flowers in leaf axils from June to September. Wasteland, hedgerows and on fences.

64   Heathlands

Heaths are rare and endangered habitats when considered worldwide – very few are found outside western Europe and most occur in Great Britain. They occur only on acid soils such as cover sandstone or granite bedrock. Here little but heather and gorse grow, and these plants, with their uniformly dark green leaves, give the heaths a very monotonous appearance except when they are in flower. In spring, the heath turns yellow with the gorse flowers, and the purple heather transforms the landscape in late summer.

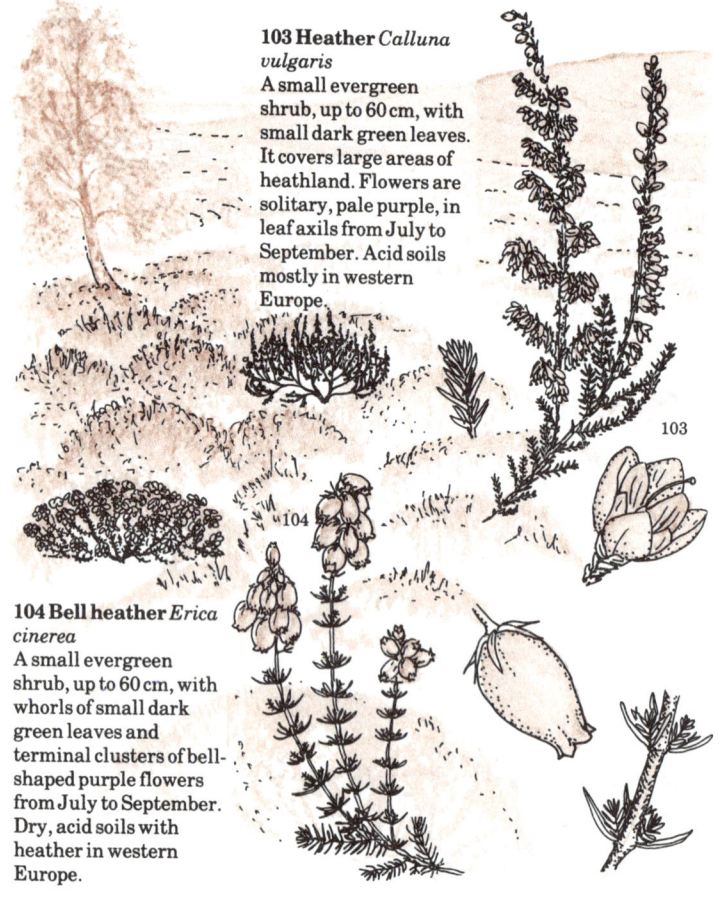

103 Heather *Calluna vulgaris*
A small evergreen shrub, up to 60 cm, with small dark green leaves. It covers large areas of heathland. Flowers are solitary, pale purple, in leaf axils from July to September. Acid soils mostly in western Europe.

104 Bell heather *Erica cinerea*
A small evergreen shrub, up to 60 cm, with whorls of small dark green leaves and terminal clusters of bell-shaped purple flowers from July to September. Dry, acid soils with heather in western Europe.

105 Gorse *Ulex europaeus*

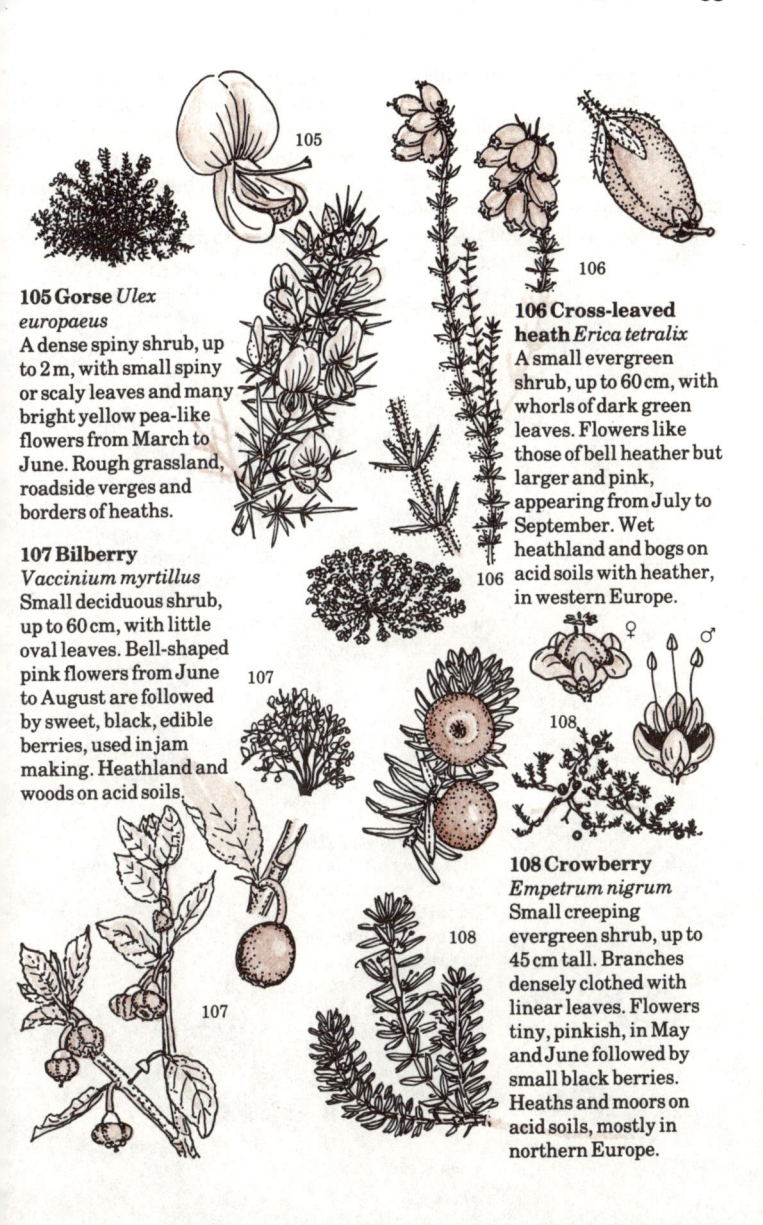

A dense spiny shrub, up to 2 m, with small spiny or scaly leaves and many bright yellow pea-like flowers from March to June. Rough grassland, roadside verges and borders of heaths.

107 Bilberry *Vaccinium myrtillus*

Small deciduous shrub, up to 60 cm, with little oval leaves. Bell-shaped pink flowers from June to August are followed by sweet, black, edible berries, used in jam making. Heathland and woods on acid soils.

106 Cross-leaved heath *Erica tetralix*

A small evergreen shrub, up to 60 cm, with whorls of dark green leaves. Flowers like those of bell heather but larger and pink, appearing from July to September. Wet heathland and bogs on acid soils with heather, in western Europe.

108 Crowberry *Empetrum nigrum*

Small creeping evergreen shrub, up to 45 cm tall. Branches densely clothed with linear leaves. Flowers tiny, pinkish, in May and June followed by small black berries. Heaths and moors on acid soils, mostly in northern Europe.

66 Grassy moorland

Upland areas with acid soils are not always covered by heather. A grassy moor may develop instead, with drier areas covered by short grasses, rather like the downs in appearance but with acid-loving plants growing there instead of lime-lovers. Many of these moors develop patches of 'moss' – wet, or at least damp, ground where cotton grass grows. In almost all of these moors the soil is peaty and, in high rainfall areas, a sphagnum bog may be present with its own very special group of plants.

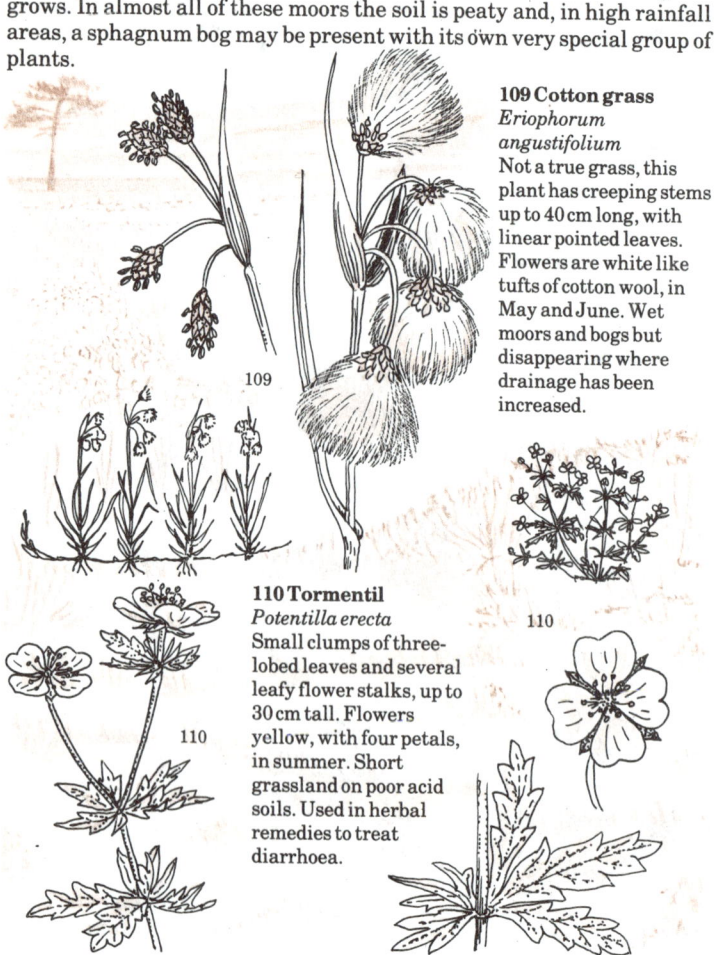

109 Cotton grass
Eriophorum angustifolium
Not a true grass, this plant has creeping stems up to 40 cm long, with linear pointed leaves. Flowers are white like tufts of cotton wool, in May and June. Wet moors and bogs but disappearing where drainage has been increased.

110 Tormentil
Potentilla erecta
Small clumps of three-lobed leaves and several leafy flower stalks, up to 30 cm tall. Flowers yellow, with four petals, in summer. Short grassland on poor acid soils. Used in herbal remedies to treat diarrhoea.

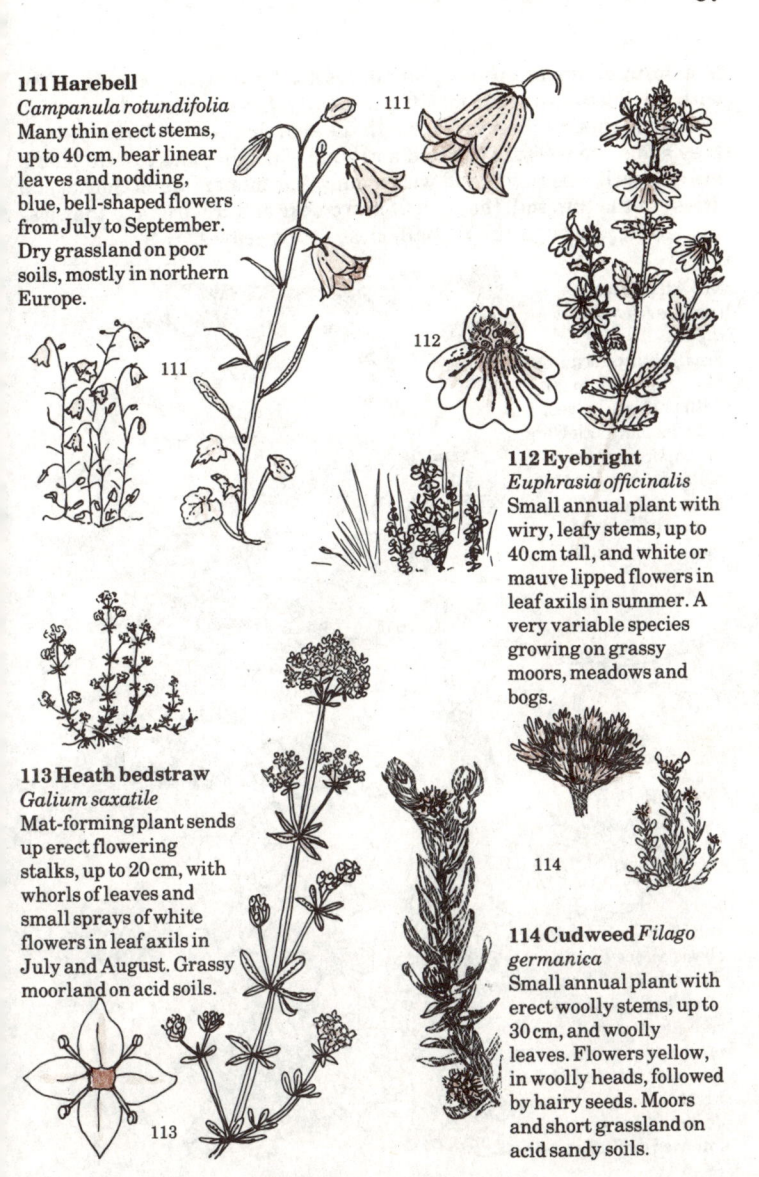

111 Harebell
Campanula rotundifolia
Many thin erect stems, up to 40 cm, bear linear leaves and nodding, blue, bell-shaped flowers from July to September. Dry grassland on poor soils, mostly in northern Europe.

112 Eyebright
Euphrasia officinalis
Small annual plant with wiry, leafy stems, up to 40 cm tall, and white or mauve lipped flowers in leaf axils in summer. A very variable species growing on grassy moors, meadows and bogs.

113 Heath bedstraw
Galium saxatile
Mat-forming plant sends up erect flowering stalks, up to 20 cm, with whorls of leaves and small sprays of white flowers in leaf axils in July and August. Grassy moorland on acid soils.

114 Cudweed *Filago germanica*
Small annual plant with erect woolly stems, up to 30 cm, and woolly leaves. Flowers yellow, in woolly heads, followed by hairy seeds. Moors and short grassland on acid sandy soils.

68 Mountains

Mountain plants are usually small, rosette-forming or creeping, often with small leaves and are mostly perennial. They are adapted to survive on the mountains sheltered beneath the snow blanket in winter, where they avoid the worst of the cold and wind. Creeping and rosette plants are also well able to contend with mountain summers when the hot sun dries out the thin soil: they can fit into cracks and crevices and they lose little water through their small, close-fitting leaves.

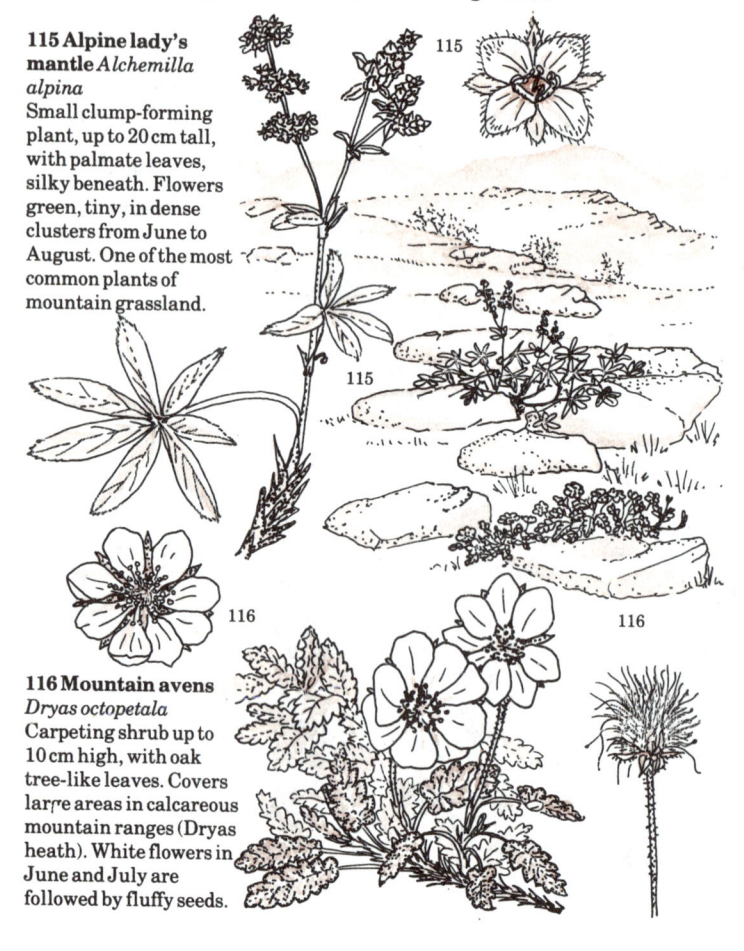

115 Alpine lady's mantle *Alchemilla alpina*
Small clump-forming plant, up to 20 cm tall, with palmate leaves, silky beneath. Flowers green, tiny, in dense clusters from June to August. One of the most common plants of mountain grassland.

116 Mountain avens *Dryas octopetala*
Carpeting shrub up to 10 cm high, with oak tree-like leaves. Covers large areas in calcareous mountain ranges (Dryas heath). White flowers in June and July are followed by fluffy seeds.

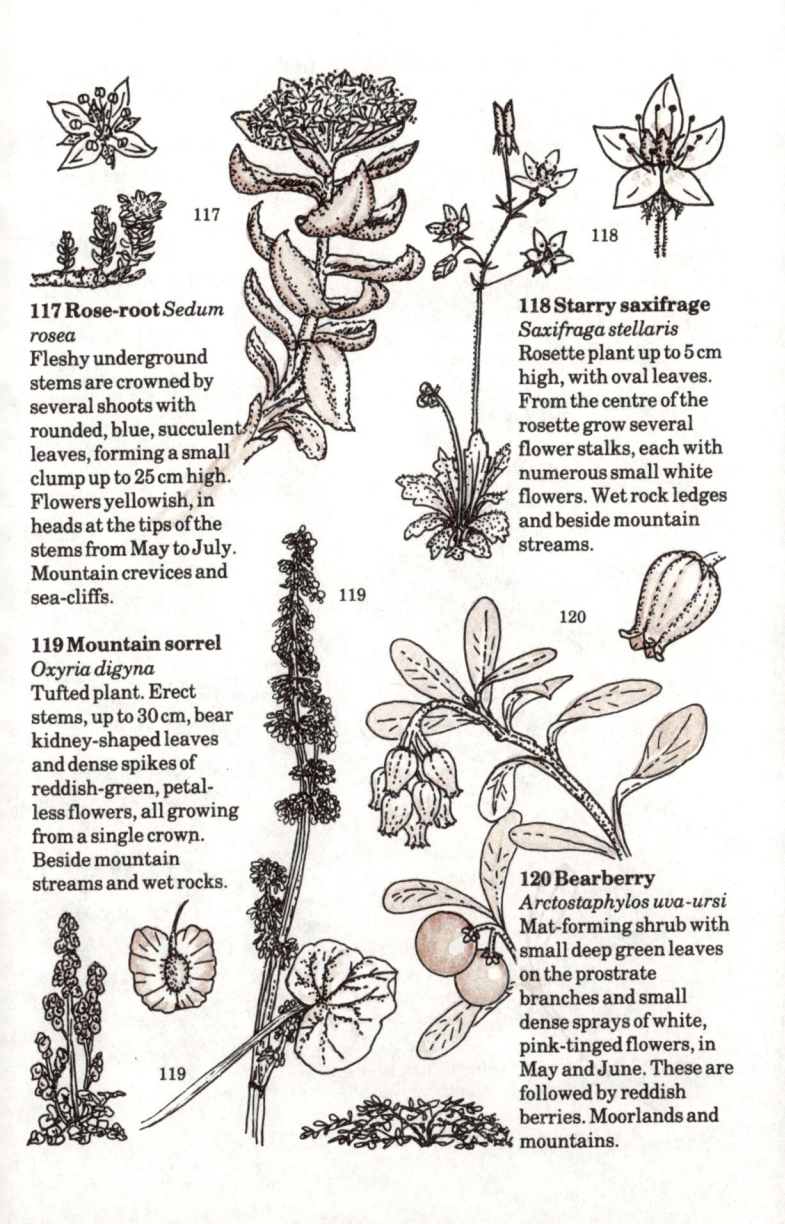

117 Rose-root *Sedum rosea*
Fleshy underground stems are crowned by several shoots with rounded, blue, succulent leaves, forming a small clump up to 25 cm high. Flowers yellowish, in heads at the tips of the stems from May to July. Mountain crevices and sea-cliffs.

118 Starry saxifrage *Saxifraga stellaris*
Rosette plant up to 5 cm high, with oval leaves. From the centre of the rosette grow several flower stalks, each with numerous small white flowers. Wet rock ledges and beside mountain streams.

119 Mountain sorrel *Oxyria digyna*
Tufted plant. Erect stems, up to 30 cm, bear kidney-shaped leaves and dense spikes of reddish-green, petal-less flowers, all growing from a single crown. Beside mountain streams and wet rocks.

120 Bearberry *Arctostaphylos uva-ursi*
Mat-forming shrub with small deep green leaves on the prostrate branches and small dense sprays of white, pink-tinged flowers, in May and June. These are followed by reddish berries. Moorlands and mountains.

70 Seashores

Few flowering plants live on the seashore in the area between the high- and low-tide levels. However, many do live just above the high-tide mark – on shingle foreshores, on sandy beaches perhaps where sand dunes begin, on rocks and cliffs, and in salt marshes (the only habitat where the plants actually grow between the tide levels). All the species are adapted to tolerate high salt intensity, to live in shifting sands or shingle, and to withstand winter storms and waves.

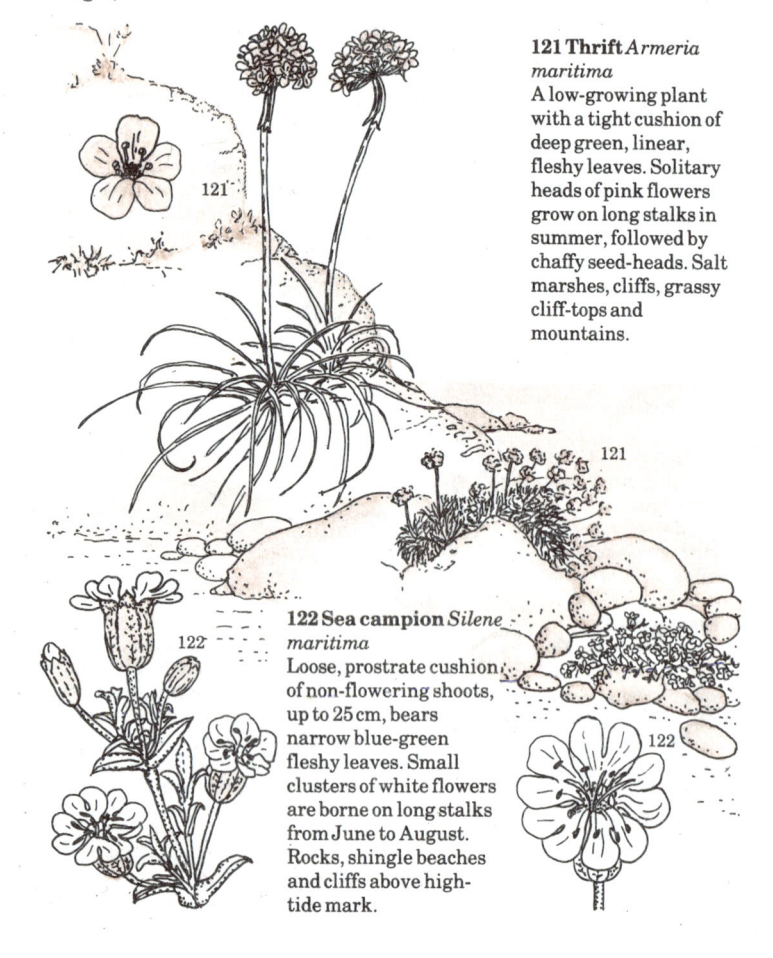

121 Thrift *Armeria maritima*
A low-growing plant with a tight cushion of deep green, linear, fleshy leaves. Solitary heads of pink flowers grow on long stalks in summer, followed by chaffy seed-heads. Salt marshes, cliffs, grassy cliff-tops and mountains.

122 Sea campion *Silene maritima*
Loose, prostrate cushion of non-flowering shoots, up to 25 cm, bears narrow blue-green fleshy leaves. Small clusters of white flowers are borne on long stalks from June to August. Rocks, shingle beaches and cliffs above high-tide mark.

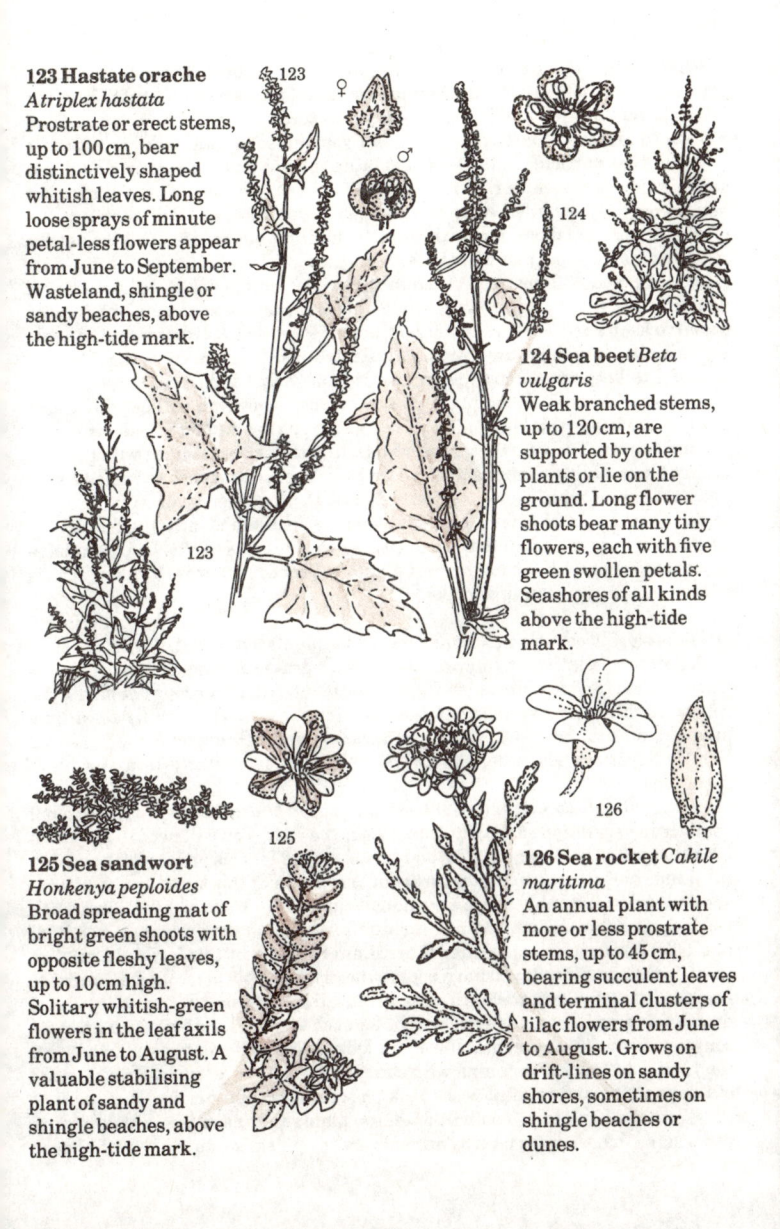

123 Hastate orache
Atriplex hastata
Prostrate or erect stems, up to 100 cm, bear distinctively shaped whitish leaves. Long loose sprays of minute petal-less flowers appear from June to September. Wasteland, shingle or sandy beaches, above the high-tide mark.

124 Sea beet *Beta vulgaris*
Weak branched stems, up to 120 cm, are supported by other plants or lie on the ground. Long flower shoots bear many tiny flowers, each with five green swollen petals. Seashores of all kinds above the high-tide mark.

125 Sea sandwort
Honkenya peploides
Broad spreading mat of bright green shoots with opposite fleshy leaves, up to 10 cm high. Solitary whitish-green flowers in the leaf axils from June to August. A valuable stabilising plant of sandy and shingle beaches, above the high-tide mark.

126 Sea rocket *Cakile maritima*
An annual plant with more or less prostrate stems, up to 45 cm, bearing succulent leaves and terminal clusters of lilac flowers from June to August. Grows on drift-lines on sandy shores, sometimes on shingle beaches or dunes.

72 Practical 1 – In the field

You have only to step out of your door and you are 'in the field'. Learning about the plants and animals in your immediate area is a first step to understanding the intricate relationships which make up the natural world. At first you may be content to identify a particular plant, but you will soon want to know why it is living in that particular place, what relationships it has with other plants and animals, how common or rare it is, and so on. For instance, a clump of stinging nettles may be regarded as a nuisance until you discover that they are the food-plant for the caterpillars of three of our loveliest butterflies. If all the nettles in your area disappear so will those butterflies.

Equipment You will not need much in the way of equipment. A comprehensive field guide to wild flowers, a magnifying glass or hand lens and a notebook and pencil to keep a record of what you find, are all essential. A camera would enable you instantly to make your record an illustrated one. A haversack or shoulder bag is useful to keep your things clean and dry and your hands free.

What to do When you find a plant that you do not know, you will need to 'run it down' in the key in this book or in the field guide. At first the botanical terms may confuse you but if you use the glossary you will soon become familiar with them (it is a bit like learning a language). You will soon realize that each term has a very precise meaning which helps to exactly describe a plant. Here a magnifying glass, or better still a hand lens, is essential since some of the identifying features of some plants are too small to be seen clearly with the naked eye. Once you have become familiar with the commonest plants in your area there are many projects or studies that you can undertake.

Projects

(1) *Habitats*. Choose one habitat and record the plants living in it. You might start with a simple, relatively uniform habitat like a grass verge on one side of a road. Once you feel confident about identifying the plants, try comparing one side of the road with the other. Complex habitats, for instance a wood on a hillside with an area of damp ground at the bottom and a track running through the centre, would provide opportunities to compare different plant communities in a variety of situations.

(2) *Seasonal variations*. You could use any habitat for a study of the seasonal changes in vegetation that occur throughout the year. You will need to choose an area that is likely to remain relatively undisturbed for this project to be successful. January is a good month to start your survey, for at this time there is little to see and you will be able to see the changes in growth from the beginning. Each week check for (a) new plants appearing from beneath the ground (b) height of plants (c) flower buds appearing (d) first flowers open – at this last point you can identify the species that you have not previously been able to recognize – (e) fruits beginning to form (f) flowering over (g) fruits all split open or dispersed (h) leaves dying. You may be able to devize graphs for each species, showing which are most conspicuous in any one month. If you carried out this study for two years then you might find differences in timing with changes in weather patterns. Keep a record of temperature and rainfall as a check on weather conditions for each season.

(3) *Plants and animals*. You will often see plants that have been eaten or with other signs that they are used by animals (galls, spiders' nests etc). A rather more

complex project would involve making a survey of the relationships between plants and insects, for instance, You would be well on your way to becoming a real naturalist at the end of such a project. The local nature conservation trust could help you learn about the relationships between plants and animals (see p. 77).

(4) *Soil types and their plants*. If you are lucky you might live in an area with several different soil types within easy reach. Your local garden society will be able to give you the details. You will find that the commonest plants grow in all areas but also that many species will be found in one kind of soil but not another.

In order to decide what soil preferences, if any, that a plant has then you need to be able to test the soil for texture and pH (a measure of how acid or alkaline the soil is). You can test for soil texture by putting a handful of soil into a jar of water and thoroughly stirring it. Sandy particles will fall to the bottom, clay will remain suspended in the water for some time, much of it finally settling out as fine silt (see also page 6).

Most soils have a mixture of sandy and clay particles – these soils are called loams. Fertile soils also have a large proportion of organic material – dead rotting leaves, twigs etc. This light material will float on the surface of the water. What kind of soil do you have in your garden? Plants are particular about soil texture but even more so about pH. You may be able to buy a soil testing kit at your local garden centre but unfortunately this is one area where progress has overtaken us – most of the garden centres are now selling pH-meters and kits for about £10.00 a time, and the old inexpensive kits with paper strips that changed colour with pH are no longer readily available. Small kits with bottles of liquid can usually be ordered but you will have to take labelled soil samples home if you have this kind of kit, since the bottles may break in the field. Instructions for using these pH kits are supplied with them. Litmus paper is available from your chemist and will give you a very rough idea of pH, changing from red in acid conditions to blue in alkaline conditions. (Make sure the soil is wet before testing it.) pH is measured on a scale from 1-14: pH 1-6 is acid, pH 7 is neutral, pH 8-14 is alkaline. Most plants prefer soil with a pH somewhere between 6-8. If the soil is more acid than this (with a low pH) or more alkaline (with a high pH), then you will find a characteristic flora of specialized plants adapted to living in such soils.

Once you have identified your type of soil, you could make a list of the plants growing in it. Suppose it is an acid soil. You would then expect to find heathlands in your area with heathers, bilberries, tormentils, bedstraws etc. There may be areas of bracken. The typical woods of acid soils are pine and birch with a ground flora of heathers, or sessile oak and beech with a ground flora of bracken and bluebells and wood anemones in spring, foxgloves and rosebay willowherb in summer. Calcareous soils (see page 6) have a much greater variety of plants. Our most widespread calcareous soils are found on the downs and limestone uplands where a wealth of sun-loving grassland species like thymes and rockroses are found. Beech woods grow on the downs and their ground flora consists of dog's mercury, violets and woodruff. Lowland calcareous soils often have English Oak and ash woods with a ground flora similar to that of the oak woods growing on acid soils but richer in species like wood anemones, primroses and violets in spring and enchanter's nightshade in summer.

Practical 2 – Keeping a record

Keeping an accurate record of field work is essential. A record acts as a constant source of information that you can use in many ways. You will know where a particular species grows, what its habitat preferences are, what time of year it is in flower, etc. Ideally you should keep a habitat record in a loose-leaf notebook, like the sample page shown opposite, cross-referenced to a species record on a card index. Then whether you need information on habitats or species you will be able to find it quickly.

Photographic records

Photographs of habitats and species add greatly to the information value of a record. You will probably find that perfectly adequate pictures for your record can be taken on the family camera. However, if you want to take high-quality pictures you will need a camera that focusses accurately down to only about 30 centimetres away from the subject. This should preferably be a single lens reflex camera so that what you see through the viewfinder is actually what you photograph. Learning to check light intensity with a light meter and focussing and adjusting the camera for different light conditions are complex actions but the results can be very rewarding. Your local camera shop will be able to help you to choose a camera that is within your price range. Choose a fast film, that is one that fixes the image quickly so that a movement will not spoil your picture; a film of ASA 400 is about right.

If possible, take your pictures between 10am and 4pm in the summer and about mid-day in spring and autumn so that shadows do not spoil your picture. If the day is very sunny, get a friend to hold a piece of white paper on the sunny side of the flower so as to make the light more uniform. You really need a completely calm day to take close-ups of flowers so if there is a breeze, be content with habitat pictures; wait for the right day to photograph your plants. If you want to take 'professional' pictures you will need a tripod on which to put your camera; a hand-held camera always moves to some extent.

Sketches

You may prefer to sketch your plants rather than photograph them and, in any event, photographs should be supplemented by sketches. A photograph cannot show the intricate details of a flower or the tooth pattern at the edge of a leaf. These may be vital to the identification of a plant species (you will know this from using the key) and a small sketch illustrates such details as words and photographs never can. You may feel that your drawing is poor but practise will soon improve your skill and, in addition, you will find yourself looking more carefully at your flowers and seeing features you never noticed before. Your observation of the habitats should improve too once you train yourself to see accurately.

How and what to record You need to record the major details of your location (time of year, type of habitat etc.) as set out at the top of the page facing, together with the object of that day's study. At first it would probably be wise to use both the common name of the plant and its Latin name, but once you get to know the plants you will be able to use the Latin name only and so save time and space. Record any necessary notes about the plants – common, in flower etc., or any obvious signs of insect damage. You will need to divide your habitat into subdivisions if you want to make comparitive studies.

Keeping a record 75

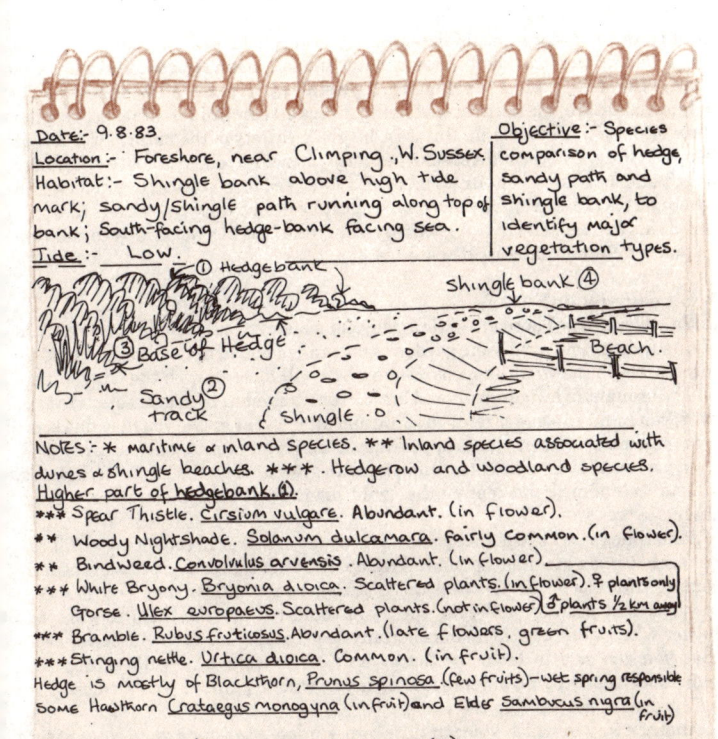

Date:- 9.8.83
Location:- Foreshore, near Climping., W. Sussex
Habitat:- Shingle bank above high tide mark; sandy/shingle path running along top of bank; South-facing hedge-bank facing sea.
Tide:- Low.

Objective:- Species comparison of hedge, sandy path and shingle bank, to identify major vegetation types.

① Hedgebank
③ Base of Hedge
② Sandy track
Shingle
Shingle bank ④
Beach.

NOTES:- * maritime & inland species. ** Inland species associated with dunes & shingle beaches. ***. Hedgerow and woodland species.

Higher part of hedgebank. ①
** Spear Thistle. Cirsium vulgare. Abundant. (in flower).
** Woody Nightshade. Solanum dulcamara. Fairly common. (in flower).
** Bindweed. Convolvulus arvensis. Abundant. (in flower)
*** White Bryony. Bryonia dioica. Scattered plants. (in flower). 2 plants only
    Gorse. Ulex europaeus. Scattered plants. (not in flower) 3 plants ½ km away
*** Bramble. Rubus fruticosus. Abundant. (late flowers, green fruits).
*** Stinging nettle. Urtica dioica. Common. (in fruit).
Hedge is mostly of Blackthorn, Prunus spinosa (few fruits) — wet spring responsible
Some Hawthorn Crataegus monogyna (in fruit) and Elder Sambucus nigra (in fruit)

Sandy track ② and base of hedge ③
* Scentless Mayweed. Tripleurospermum maritimum. Abundant ③ (in flower).
* Sea Beet. Beta vulgaris. Abundant ③. (in flower).
** Ragwort. Senecio jacobaea. Common ③ (in flower).
* Yellow Horned Poppy. Glaucium flavum. Locally common ③. (in fruit).

Shingle bank ④.
** Hastate Orache. Atriplex hastata. Abundant. (in flower).
* Sea Cabbage. Crambe maritima. Large patches of plants.
** Woody Nightshade. Solanum dulcamara. Patchy. (in flower).
* Yellow Horned Poppy. Glaucium flavum. Patchy — same as '82. (in fruit).
* Scentless Mayweed. Tripleurospermum maritum ssp. maritimum.
    Very common. (in flower) NB. Smaller plants than in hedge.
* Sea Sandwort. Honkenya peploides. 2 large spreading patches.
** Curled Dock. Rumex crispus. Scattered, especially around rocks. (in fruit).

Practical 3 – Conservation

The desire for conservation of the natural world is not a sentimental one. We, as people, are just as dependent on clean water and soil, clean air, good food and space as any other living thing. What makes it possible for us to live on this planet is the balance of nature, the multitude of living things all doing different tasks, keeping the world fit for all to live in. But it is the great variety of the natural world that keeps it going. Every time a species becomes extinct its role in the web of life may be left undone. So to keep our world healthy we need to stop the extinctions which we ourselves are continually causing, usually by destroying the habitats in which the plants and animals live. A good way of maintaining our world is by conserving as many different habitats as possible.

What can you do?
(1) *In your garden* There are several ways in which you can help to conserve wild plants (and animals) in your garden. You can leave one area wild. It should be interesting to see what happens. Some seeds will blow in with the wind, others will be brought in by mammals and birds. If one common species threatens to take over, you could do some careful weeding and after a year or two you may find some less common species of plants appearing. Even if you cannot leave an area wild, then you could still leave some wild plants to grow around the garden; foxgloves, violets, celandines and many other wild plants will seed themselves without taking over.

Sometimes a strange plant appears as a clump of leaves in the spring and it can be fascinating watching the plant develop, growing flower buds and eventually coming into bloom. Do not pull these strangers up, unless they are in a very inconvenient position and even then you could try moving them to some odd corner where they can do no harm. Many seed catalogues list wild flower seeds that you can sow in lawns or flower beds, or in your own wild garden. But remember not to dig up plants growing in the wild to plant in your garden. They will probably not survive the move.

Another way in which you can turn your garden into your own private nature reserve is to stop using poisons. You can write to the Henry Doubleday Association for ways of controlling pests in your garden without using poisons and for methods of organic gardening. You will find that a poison-free garden has many more wild plants and insects than one in which modern chemicals are used and your garden plants will also benefit since you will not be killing off all the predator insects.

(2) *In the field* You may have noticed that there is no reference to pressed flowers in this book. To press a flower you have to pick it and conservationists would prefer to encourage you to enjoy it growing in its own chosen home, rather than killing it. It is illegal to uproot wild plants, and if a plant is on the protected plant list, it is illegal even to pick the flowers. Photographs and sketches provide more permanent souvenirs of a plant spotting expedition than do dying flowers. So conserve the wild plants in your area by leaving them where they are and encouraging others to do the same. And remember – watch where you put your feet. An unwary footstep can cause a great deal of damage to seedlings and young plants and some species cannot survive being trampled.

Conservation

Organizations to join
There are several conservation organizations that you can join, either as an individual or as a member of a group such as a school class, guides or scouts etc. Your teacher might be interested – why not ask?

The Royal Society for Nature Conservation (RSNC) has county groups or trusts in most of the counties of the UK. You can find the address of your county trust by writing to the RSNC at the address given below. Each county trust is split into area groups. They run nature walks and films shows, raise funds and organize working parties to maintain local nature reserves and areas of local interest. One of the most important tasks undertaken by the county trusts is raising funds to buy special sites threatened by development, wetlands threatened by drainage, woodlands threatened by tree cutting etc. If you take an active role in such a trust you will really be helping to conserve wild plants and animals.

The junior branch of the RSNC is called Watch; there are Watch groups all over the country. There may be one near you – your county trust will know – and if there is not one, someone in your school or area may be willing to help set one up. Watch groups carry out all sorts of exciting projects from Frogwatch (a rescue and survey study of frogs) to Tree Race (a tree planting program), sponsored butterfly counts, dragonfly surveys and painting competitions. Conservation is important, so get involved! Below is a list of addresses which will be of help.

Useful addresses
1) Royal Society for Nature Conservation, The Green, Nettleham, Lincoln LN2 2NR.

2) Nature Conservancy Council, Interpretative Branch, Attingham Park, Shrewsbury SY4 4TW.
Government body responsible for nature conservation. Information is available on sites of special interest and nature trails.

3) Forestry Commission, 231 Corstorphine Road, Edinburgh EH12 7AT.
Runs wildlife and nature trails in forestry areas.

4) Countryside Commission, John Dower House, Crescent Place, Cheltenham, Gloucester GL50 3RA.
Provides information on national and country parks.

5) Henry Doubleday Research Association, 20 Convent Lane, Bocking, Braintree, Essex.
Provides information and materials for poison-free gardens.

Recommended sites

Wherever you go, you will find wild plants growing. Small woods, hedgerows and roadside verges are often rich in the commoner species. But to see the less common species and the rarities you will have to visit the classic areas for plant spotting, many of which are listed below.

South and South-west England

Area	*Habitat*
1) New Forest (Hampshire)	woodland and heathland flora
2) Chalk Downs of many southern counties	downland flora
3) Torbay area (Devon)	limestone flora
4) The Lizard (Cornwall)	heathland flora
5) Scilly Isles	these islands, together with Devon, Cornwall and Pembroke, contain plants belonging to the Lusitanian flora of southern Europe, which are generally rare in Britain.

Midlands, East Anglia and North-east England

1) Brecklands of Norfolk and Suffolk	sandy heaths with a unique flora
2) Broads and fens of East Anglia	water and waterside plants.
3) Upper Teesdale (Durham)	limestone and alpine flora
4) Yorkshire Pennines, especially Craven Limestone	acid moors and woods; limestone uplands and limestone pavement

Wales, Western and North-west England

1) Forest of Dean (Gloucester)	oak and beech woodland
2) Lake District	mountain area with arctic-alpine flora
3) Snowdonia (Caernarvon)	mountain area with arctic-alpine flora
4) Great Orme Head (Caernarvon)	limestone flora
5) Gower Peninsular (South Wales)	limestone flora

Scotland

1) Grampian mountains, especially Ben Lawers	high moorland and mountains; arctic-alpine flora
2) Western Highlands	many mountains each with their own arctic-alpine specialities
3) Machair (Western and Northern Isles)	specialized lime-loving plants on machair dunes

Ireland

1) Highlands of Kerry and Cork	Lusitanian species
2) The Burren (Co. Clare)	limestone karst area with a unique assemblage of arctic and Mediterranean species
3) Ben Bulben Range (Sligo)	mountain arctic-alpine flora
4) Connemara and western Mayo	heaths and mountains with mixed Lusitanian and Irish-American flora

Coastal habitats including dunes, shingle banks, sea-cliffs, salt-marshes etc., are particularly rich in species in Kent, Essex, Norfolk, Western and Northern Isles, Anglesey, Gower Peninsular, western coast of Ireland.

Further reading/Glossary/Index

Blamey, M., *Flowers of the Countryside*. Collins 1980.
Clapham, A. R., Tutin, T. G. and Warburg, E. F. *Excursion Flora of the British Isles*. Third Ed. Cambridge University Press 1981.
Field guide to the Wild Flowers of Britain. Reader's Digest 1981.
Fitter, R. S. R. *Finding Wild Flowers*. A practical handbook to plant-hunting in Britain and a county-by-county guide. Collins 1971.
Gilmour, J. and Walters, M. *Wild Flowers*. Fifth Ed. Collins, New Naturalists 1973.
Phillips, R. *Wild Flowers of Britain*. Pan 1977.
Schauer, T. *Field Guide to the Wild Flowers of Britain and Europe*. Collins 1982.
Tebbs, B. *Guide to Wild Flowers of Britain and Europe*. Usborne 1981.

Glossary

This is not a true glossary but more a cross between a glossary and a subject index. Where botanical terms are explained elsewhere in the book, page references are given instead of explanations.

Annual plants: see page 15
Biennial plants: see page 15
Crown: The neck of a clump-forming plant, usually at or just beneath ground level
Flower arrangements: see pages 16-17
Flower parts: see pages 14-15
Flower types: see pages 15, 16-17
Fruits: see page 17
Habitat: The place where a particular plant or animal lives.
Leaf arrangements: see pages 16-17
Leaf axil: The V-shaped junction between a leaf or leaf-stalk and a stem.
Leaf shapes: see pages 16-17
Perennial plants: see page 15
Sap: The juice inside stems and leaves.
Soil types: see pages 6, 73
Spathe: A sheath-like structure enclosing a flower or leaf.

Index

Aaron's rod 39
Alkanet 27
Anemone, wood 30
Angelica, wild 33
Arrowhead 12, 19
Asphodel, bog 20
Avens
   mountain 68
   wood 23
Bearberry 69
Bedstraw
   heath 67
   lady's 13, 45
Beet, sea 13, 71
Bellflower, large 27
Bilberry 65

Bindweed 13, 28
   greater 63
Bistort, amphibious 12, 53
Bluebell 7, 30
Brooklime 50
Bugle 33
Bulrush 12, 48
Burdock 61
Burnet, salad 45
Butterbur 12, 49
Buttercup
   creeping 59
   meadow 42
Campion
   red 34
   sea 13, 70

Cat's ear 39
Celandine
   greater 22
   lesser 35
Centaury 27
Charlock 54
Chervil, rough 36
Chickweed
   common 56
   mouse-ear 24
Cinquefoil, creeping 39
Cleavers 37
Clover
   red 43
   white 43
Codlins and cream 12, 49

Index

Columbine 23
Comfrey 12, 47
Cotton grass 66
Cowberry 26
Cowslip 43
Cranesbill
  cut-leaved 61
  dove's foot 17
Crowberry 65
Crowfoot, water 12, 53
Cuckoo flower 46
Cudweed 67
Daffodil 20
Daisy
  common 58
  ox-eye 42
Dandelion 58
Dead-nettle, white 17
Dock
  broad-leaved 26
  curled 62
Dog's mercury 31
Duckweed 12, 52
Elder, ground 59
Eyebright 67
Fat hen 57
Figwort 28
Flag
  sweet 12, 19
  yellow 12, 48, 49
Flax, purging 24
Forget-me-not, water 12, 51
Foxglove 32
Fumitory
  common 55
  yellow 41
Gorse 65
Groundsel 56
Hardheads 45
Harebell 67
Hawkweed 63
Heath, cross-leaved 65
Heather
  common 64
  bell 64
Henbane 28
Herb Robert 37
Hogweed 25
Jack-by-the-hedge 37
Knotgrass 13, 57
Lady's mantle, alpine 68
Lavender, sea 26
Loosestrife, purple 12, 49
Lords and ladies 35
Lousewort 47
Madder, field 29
Mallow
  common 63
  marsh 25

Marigold, marsh 12, 51
Marram grass 13
Mayweed, scentless 13, 55
Meadowsweet 12, 48
Milfoil *see* Yarrow
Mint, water 51
Monkey flower 12, 51
Montbretia 20
Nettle, stinging 62, 72
Nightshade
  enchanter's 22
  woody 63
Nipplewort 29
Orache
  common 13, 61
  hastate 71
Orchid
  pyramidal 17
  spotted 47
Pansy, field 55
Parsley
  cow 36
  hedge 36
Pellitory-of-the-wall 21
Pennywort, wall 41
Pepper, wall 40
Pimpernel
  scarlet 55
  yellow 27
Pineapple weed 60
Plantain
  great 21
  water 12, 53
Policeman's helmet 12, 61
Pondweed
  broad-leaved 52
  curled 12, 19
Poppy, field 54
Primrose 35
Ragged robin 12, 46
Ragwort 13, 38
Ramsons 31
Reedmace, lesser 19
Restharrow 13, 24
Ribwort 59
Rockrose, common 44
Rose-root 69
Sandwort, sea 13, 71
Saxifrage
  purple 23
  starry 69
Scabious
  devil's bit 47
  field 29
Sea rocket 13, 71
Seablite, herbaceous 21
Self-heal 28, 29
Shepherd's purse 57
Snowdrop 7

Sorrel
  common 43
  mountain 69
  upright yellow 25
  wood 31
Spearwort, lesser 50
Speedwell, germander 59
Spurge
  petty 21
  sun 57
Stitchwort, greater 34
St. John's wort, perforate 33
Stonecrop, white 16, 26
Storksbill 13, 25
Strawberry
  barren 17
  wild 33
Thistle
  creeping 39
  spear 60
Thrift 70
Thyme 13, 44
Toadflax, ivy-leaved 40
Tormentil 66
Trefoil, bird's foot 45
Tutsan 24
Twayblade 20
Valerian
  common 29
  red 41
Vetch, bush 37
Violet
  common 31
  sweet 23
Water lily
  white 12, 52
  yellow 12, 22
Whitlow grass 41
Willowherb, rosebay 32
Wintercress 12, 22
Woodruff 17
Wormwood, sea 13, 17
Woundwort, hedge 35
Yarrow 38